# Reflections on Blackpool

## Terry Potter

**This edition published by Book Clearance Centre, 1999**

Whilst every effort has been made to ensure that the information given in this book is correct, neither the publisher nor the author accept any responsibility for any inaccuracy.

**British Library Cataloguing in Publication Data**

A CIP record for this book is available from the British Library.

**Former ISBN:** 1-85058-425-7

**Cover photograph:** Blackpool and its tower, at the turn of the century; see page 112.

**Printed and bound by:** MFP Design & Print

# Contents

# 1

# The Birth of Blackpool

Although it is generally agreed that Blackpool's attempts to attract visitors started in the late 18th century – in 1788 it was reported that there were six houses 'appropriated for the reception of company' – by 1840 there were still no more houses on the sea front than about 20, according to one writer (Pevsner), and it was the coming of the railway in the 1840s that boosted Blackpool into life. Between then and the turn of the century the rate of progress was staggering. Although the original Uncle Tom's Cabin dated to 1750 – more on that place elsewhere – it was within a year or two of a century later that the semblance of modern Blackpool began to take shape.

Lists of dates are anathema to many readers but sometimes do illustrate in the best way just how fast progress can be. Gas lighting was introduced in 1852, Sacred Heart RC Church, Talbot Street, came in 1857 to cater to the needs of a substantial Roman Catholic part of the population, the earliest record of a fire brigade is to be found a year later, and in 1863 the North Pier – the oldest of the three – opened. That year also saw Central Station built (it closed in the 1960s). This encouraged hordes of visitors and is now the site of some of Blackpool's most modern redevelopment.

In 1864, piped water was introduced. Christ Church, Abingdon Street, was built the following year, and in 1868 the Central Pier was opened, to be followed two years later by the opening of the Promenade. The year 1876 saw one of the greatest days in the town's life when it was granted its Charter of Incorporation, the first Mayor being W.H. Cocker, and the borough's facilities advanced at an ever-quickening rate: 1878 – fire station built in Hull Street; 1878 – St. John's Church, Church Street; 1878 – Winter Gardens opened as 'Winter Gardens and Open Air Skating Rink; 1879 – World's first electric arc street lighting; 1883 – All Hallows Church, All Hallows Road; 1885 – world's first permanent electric street tramway opened, Cocker Street to South Shore; 1885 – Blackpool Co-operative Society formed; 1888 – Rawcliffe Street Methodist Church; 1891 – United Trades and Labour Council of Blackpool and District; 1893 – South Pier opened; 1894 –

Tower opened; 1894 – Grand Theatre opened; 1894 – Sacred Heart RC Church, Talbot Road, enlarged; 1894 – Holy Trinity Church, Dean Street; 1895 – start of building of Town Hall (opened 1900); 1896 – Gigantic Wheel opened; 1898 – St. Paul's Church, Dickson Road, North Shore; 1899 – Tower Ballroom. But enough of dates, for they become tedious. Suffice to say that this random selection from the breathless rush of development illustrates that the town knew it was really going places.

From the 1840s most visitors arrived by railway which, even though the carriages were pretty primitive, was a blessing when compared with the transport that had to be suffered by the first visitors to Blackpool. The historian J.J. Bagley states of the 1780s: 'It was not easy to reach the Lancashire resorts. In the 1780s two or three coaches were running a thrice-weekly summer service from Manchester to Blackpool, but each carried a mere dozen passengers and charged 13s 6d for the single journey. By the turn of the century, a few coaches, usually one a week during the season, were taking holiday-makers to Blackpool from the bigger West Riding towns, but even after 1816, when a daily coach service first linked Preston and Blackpool, most visitors continued to arrive on their own cart or chaise, on horseback or on foot.'

So it came as a mighty big relief when the Preston to Fleetwood Railway opened in 1840 and was extended from Poulton-le-Fylde to Blackpool six years later. The flood of trippers did not slow and Blackpool boomed, so much so that by the turn of the century it had ambitions to become a County Borough, an ambition that was realised on October 1, 1904. The next 21 years were a particularly busy time in the resort's growth. The population grew from about 50,000 to about 100,000 and the rateable value from around £400,000 to £1,000,000 – and the importance of Blackpool was becoming widely recognised.

King George and Queen Mary visited in 1913, the Duchess Louise and Duke of Argyle in 1912, and the Prince of Wales in 1921. The standard of building for the town centre had already been set by the Winter Gardens complex. This was crucial to the development of Blackpool, for the style stamped its mark on all around it and also made the point that there was to be no stinting on expenditure. It is indeed a glorious group – Pavilion, 1878: £107,000; Empress Ballroom, 1897: £130,000. That was big money and the dreams of the town were big and lasting. From 1894 until the building of

*Directory of Westmorland and Lonsdale with Amounderness, P. Mannes, 1851:* In the last 15 years great improvements have been effected at Blackpool in the laying out of new streets and walks, the erection of the handsome houses and shops, the establishment of elegant hotels, news and billiards rooms, etc., and the building of St John's Market, which has supplied to the place a great desideratum.

*A rather desultory scene on the Promenade from a postcard post-marked October 22, 1905. The Tower is just visible on the left. The card is addressed to a Miss A. Tomlinson, c/o Miss Richard, Regent Point, Lancaster, and despite bearing a half-penny stamp, has the somewhat cryptic message: 'Dear Alice, – No one will know if you do not tell them that this has not been through the post. I am on the cheap side again like you. Do not let any one see the above you see I am not in work like you earning you pennies and I do not like asking mother every time for a stamp unless I am forced. It is signed 'from your sister Maggie' and also comments, 'Your turn now.'*

QUEENS HOTEL, HYDRO. & PROMENADE, BLACKPOOL

*Manchester Mercury*, June 3, 1783: The Manchester and Blackpool coach from the Upper Royal Oak, Market Street Lane, Manchester, begins to run on Monday, the 9th of June, and every morning (Sunday excepted) at 6 O'clock, through Bolton, Chorley, Preston, etc

the Post Office Tower in London, Blackpool's Tower was the highest building in Britain. Other notable events during this time included the opening of the Carnegie Library in 1911, the promotion of two great aviation meetings in 1909 and 1910, the amalgamation of Blackpool and Bispham, Blackpool becoming a Parliamentary borough in 1917, the purchase of the Blackpool and Fleetwood trams in 1919.

Early years saw many problems, of course, with a peaks and troughs cycle being much in evidence. After the turn of the century money was particularly tight in the aftermath of the Boer War but, showing a zealous faith in the future, big schemes were put through by the Corporation, including the major step of the widening of the Promenade, something that had been talked about for years. In June, 1901, the Highways Committee decided on a 60 ft. widening, the work to start at the end of the

*An evocative card postmarked December 1905, showing simple wooden boarding down to the beach, donkeys and horses and, extreme right, a policeman keeping an eye on things.*

season, but only a few days later the whole Council decided that would not be enough and put the figure at 100 ft. And the scheme was particularly welcome, for these were lean times indeed, all North West resorts experiencing the post-war slump. After the Boer War the building trade laid off thousands of workers and many had to resort to charity and the soup kitchens. Of Blackpool, the *Visitor* newspaper commented: 'There are already many at work to whom the handling of a pick and shovel is a novel experience, but in the present state of things any work is accepted and groups of men are to be seen daily gazing upon those who are fortunate enough to be in work.'

## Rivals

The rival town, home of that newspaper, was not crowing. In Morecambe itself building had virtually come to a halt, some part-built houses being left with roofs open to the elements. Blackpool got the final official go-ahead for the

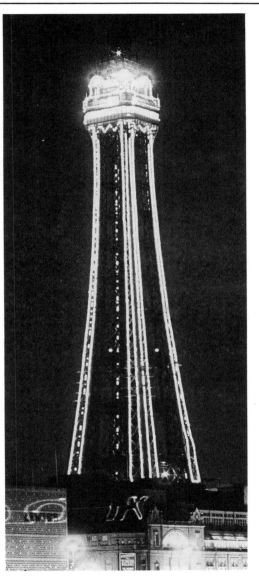

*The Tower, epitome of Blackpool, opened in 1894.*

Promenade widening the following January and decided to start at once. It is to the credit of the 'city fathers' that the Corporation of the time was making massive efforts to advertise the charms of Blackpool. Their declared intention was to get a poster of the resort on every hoarding in the United Kingdom and in 1902 they turned their attention to the Continent. French and Swiss railway stations and resorts were the main target. But the lean times continued. In December, 1902, public subscriptions flooded in for a Mayor's Distress Fund, a feature of Blackpool that was familiar for many years.

The Census returns of these turn of the century years are revealing: 1881 – 14,229; 1891 – 24,846; 1901 – 47,346. A trebling in a period of 20 years or so. In fact, the population of all the towns· in the North West with ambitions to being resorts were increasingly rapidly and Blackpool's task was to stay ahead of the game. The little town of St. Annes, which started the decade with a population of only 588, had doubled itself again and again and in 1901 boasted an eminently respectable 6,838 – something more than 11 times the figure of 1891. Lytham had increased by about a third since 1891, bringing it to 7,185. Fleetwood in the 1901 Census returned a figure of 12,093 – an increase of 2,819 on the ten years. It must be remembered, however, that these figures referred only to the compact boroughs or districts of those days, which were much smaller in area than they are now.

Not all visitors to Blackpool occupied the seemingly endless streets of hotels and guesthouses. The early stirrings of the holiday camp trade were taking place and in 1906, for instance, no fewer than 52 bell tents and marquees were reported to be found on the Norbreck Cliffs, overlooking the sea, let to holidaymakers who wished to cultivate the simple life at one guinea per head per week.

As the first decade of the 20th century approached its close, Blackpool was thinking increasingly about the physical appearance of the town. The year 1909 saw several schemes to put a gloss on the resort. Thousands of pounds were spent on tree planting and open spaces and plans were put in the 'in tray' for a large car park to help rid the Promenade of the congestion that was already becoming a daily nuisance, and for municipal bowling greens and tennis courts. It all added up to a considerable policy of beautification. For many years the Corporation had wanted to extend the Promenade from the North Pier round by the Metropole to Claremont

Park and in 1910 they decided to go ahead, at a cost of about £339,000.

One of the most luxurious and comfortable Hotels in the world. Stands in own grounds on the Sea Front, in the centre of the beautiful Princess Promenade.

Could such growth be sustained? Many towns could not have kept up the pace but in Blackpool's case the answer was 'yes', but in 1914 the First World War intervened and there was a natural, if not very big, lull in the frantic pace of building that had become the norm. The town remained busy throughout the war and afterwards there was a resurgence of effort in major schemes in not only Blackpool but the other Northern resorts. Blackpool's task again was to stay ahead of the game. Only a few miles away, at Morecambe, one of its chief rivals, there were so-called 'new blood' council elections which resulted in a new progressiveness. It is instructive to see what was the opposition to Blackpool.

*The Metropole, one of Blackpool's best-known hotels, advertises itself in 1920. Saturday to Monday from 37 shillings – not bad value!*

*Wishful thinking in Blackpool?*

If I only had the Cash I'd show you How to swank at Blackpool.

On the resort's doorstep, Lytham and St. Annes announced plans for building a sea wall, marine lake, open-air baths and to build the Blackpool, St. Annes and Lytham Tramways Co. Ltd. At Filey the Council announced plans to extend, enclose and alter the Crescent Gardens and South Crescent Gardens to create 'grounds for cricket and other games, sports meetings, assemblies, bowling greens, tennis courts, skating rinks and croquet lawns,' ornamental gardens with pavilions, bandstands, reading rooms and a host of other attractions – quite impressive for a town with a population of only about 3,200. Scarborough decided to make a major promotion of crown green bowling, to build 32 more 'bathing boxes' and 12 bungalows. At Bridlington, ratepayers at a town's meeting approved, 'by an overwhelming majority,' plans for whole new streets and street improvements, to extend the Prince's Parade, and to run omnibuses. Skegness embarked on major plans for the development of the sea shore and promenade gardens, which the Council had bought from the Earl

F_46125. BLACKPOOL: THE FLAGSTAFF, PRINCESS PARADE.

*Little change in 80 years: the Tower still occupies central position in this postcard of Princess Parade.*

of Scarborough. Included were a six-acre bathing pool, 50 bungalows, tennis courts, golf putting, croquet and bowling greens, sports enclosure of seven acres, children's playground, boating lake, a 'chine' fairground and 'numerous ornamental shelters and kiosks'.

The money had to be found – but money was being made. In 1920 at Blackpool, for the privilege of letting that most ubiquitous of seaside objects, the deckchair, in the borough for a term of three years a woman was prepared to pay £600 for the first year, £625 for the second and £650 for the third. But after what was described as a 'breezy debate,' Blackpool Corporation decided on letting the chairs themselves. All the resorts continued to expand at an impressive rate. In 1922 it was reported of Southport that due to the amount of building 'effective supervision could not be carried out by the building inspector with an ordinary bicycle' and it was decided to get him a motorcycle. In March, 1923, over 300 plans were laid before Blackpool's Building Plans Committee, 212 of which were approved, and the total for the year so far had been 316. Builders were becoming more confident, plans only for single or two or three houses giving way to whole estates. Perhaps a surprise with all this development was that the rates in Blackpool did not go sky-high. Indeed, in 1924, at seven shillings in the £, the resort's rate was reported as being the lowest of any county borough in the country. There is no doubt that successful municipal trading was one of the ingredients of Blackpool's rates success. In 1923, for instance, a record profit of £73,000 was made, £25,000 of which was devoted to rates relief.

But perhaps the most important ingredient of Blackpool's success has been that it has never pretended to be anything other than what it is – bright and breezy. Attempts have often been made to control the extremes of this marketplace approach to life, and in the past this applied particularly to traders and entertainers on the sands. In the first decade of the century there was endless trouble with the sands operators – not the least of the Council's problems being to get them to pay the rents for their pitches. In April, 1905, the Council decided that in future those who held pitches should pay half the rent down

and the other half later. Councillors had every right to be concerned. They were still owed £200 from the previous year, with little chance of recouping the money. Not surprisingly, they decided that no licences would be granted to those in arrears. Only a month earlier the Watch Committee was told by one Councillor Bancroft that he wanted 'no quacks, corn doctors or hair kings' on the sands. The meeting heartily concurred and voted accordingly.

Of course, the story of Blackpool is-one of endless schemes and dreams and the history of the resort is littered with 'busted' concerns. An apparently endless supply of old pictures of steamships at the piers packed with trippers, fails to recall that running the steamship companies was a complex and tough business. A particularly well-known company, the North Pier Steamship Company, went into liquidation in 1905 and had to sell its fleet, including the Greyhound, Belle and Clifton. Rivals, the Blackpool Passenger Steamboat Company, gleefully took over the service. They were already sailing from the Central Pier and more than welcomed the opportunity to take over the North Pier sailings.

## Keeping an eye on morals

While Blackpool boomed there were, as

Three Promenades, North Shore, Blackpool

*Something to be proud of: three promenades, North Shore.*

always, those who looked with disdainful eye at some of the goings-on and self-appointed guardians of the public morals were much in evidence. This applied particularly to that pernicious feature of the new age – the picture postcard. In 1912 a group of local worthies decided to organise themselves into a censorship committee. They issued a circular to shopkeepers asking for co-operation and also write to manufacturers of picture postcards asking them to submit new designs to the committee before putting them on sale.

The idea was that the cards would bear an official stamp of approval. The scheme appears to have been short-lived and to have been signally unsuccessful, but similar sentiments are expressed to the present day. Twenty years later the Chief Constable of Blackpool, H.E. Derham, reported that the police had examined 16,500 'comic postcards' but only a few had been found to be 'vulgar.'

*What the well-dressed lady visitor to Blackpool would have worn in the 1920s (Daily Mail, March 10, 1924.*

These had been withdrawn or seized. I wonder what he would have thought about some of today's cards! The naughty picture postcard continues as one of the great traditions of the British Seaside. The danger of sinking into high farce as guardian of the public morals had been illustrated as early as 1884, when the moral dangers inherent in bathing in the sea had exercised the minds of councillors. In February of that year they decided that their beach inspectors should have telescopes. Apparently there had been reports of 'men bathing at certain places without drawers on.'

Such goings-on could not be countenanced, of course. The problem was to catch the offenders in the act. On this particular occasion an inspector, having been told of drawer-less bathing men, had not been able to verify the scene with the naked eye and had wasted much time by hurrying there, only to find the men correctly attired. Telescopes at the ready from now on!

One of the biggest areas of change in the early years of the present century was that which ultimately became the Golden Mile, which is land reclaimed from the sea when the Promenade was widened. Houses and shops were often invaded by the sea in Winter, so the Promenade was widened towards the sea, the scheme being largely the brainchild of a brilliant surveyor of Blackpool, James Brodie, a man who had utter belief in the town's success. There was a double bonus for the resort through this work. Not only did the new security from the waves take shape but thousands of trippers came specially to Blackpool to watch the immense building operations. Hundreds of men were employed on the scheme. This Golden Mile area had been one of solid respectable terraced houses with long front gardens. What a difference there was to be a few years later.

*The Imperial, one of Blackpool's most prestigious hotels, advertises in 1934.*

## Parks and Gardens

Some idea of the state of parts of the town can be gleaned from learning that the area now occupied by the glory that is Stanley Park boasted the charms of pig sties, brickworks and old dilapidated buildings. The Park was the product of Blackpool's first major planning scheme off the Promenade and sea front. In 1920 the state of the land was shameful to the burgeoning resort which needed some beautiful open spaces as 'lungs' for its ever- increasing population. Sir Lindsay Parkinson took a lead by buying a large portion of the derelict land and selling it at cost to the Council. Other land was compulsorily purchased and smaller areas were given by other worthies so that eventually there was nearly 300 acres o beautify.

Who better to entrust with the work than Thomas H. Mawson, the architect born in Scorton, near Garstang who had risen to become one of the pre-eminent landscape artists of the day, with prospering offices in Lancaster and London, successful international contracts in Greece, Canada, the USA, and some particularly noted work back at home in the Lake District? Mawson made an outstanding job of Stanley Park, with its 22-acre lake, and it is interesting to read what he says of the work in his sought-after autobiography, *The Life and Works of an English Landscape Architect*:

*'For years I had been distressed in contemplating the baneful results of the lack of logical planning manifested in our seaside resorts, which suffer by comparison with those on the Continent and in America. Here at least the aesthetic possibilities should be made to influence the visitors educationally. It may appear strange that in all the town planning work of which I have dreamed, Blackpool appealed to me the most. The fact that I am a Lancashire man may account for this preference. Blackpool's unbroken stretch of golden sand, its bracing air, and the kaleidoscopic gaiety of its miles of promenade, combine to weave a spell of attraction.*

*'Already, according to the town's present configuration, the streets and railway terminals of the popular resort are taxed to their fullest capacity, with a resident and visitor population of 300,000. If the Borough is to expand, as the Council anticipate, to accommodate over a million people, drastic alterations will be necessary. At present the expansion of the town is more rapid than that of any other town in the kingdom. Blackpool's phenomenal growth necessitates the provision of at least a thousand new homes a year, a fact which proves that a vast residential population is settling within the boundaries of the town. This, be it remembered, in addition to the increasing influx of visitors. When these facts are taken into consideration, it will be inferred that a thorough overhauling of the design of this great Lancashire holiday resort is demanded.'*

Mawson goes on to describe how in July, 1922, he received a letter from the Town Clerk informing him that the

New Savoy Hotel and Cliff Gardens, Blackpool.

*An early postcard from the days of virtually-empty roads.*

Council had bought 280 acres of land for a park and recreation ground and that they wished Mawson to carry out the development. Stanley Park, opened officially by Lord Derby on October 2, 1926, was a stunning success.

In a note in his autobiography, published in 1927, Mawson comments: 'The annual income from the park has already exceeded our estimates,' and he did such a splendid job that the Council used him, working with the Borough Engineer, Francis Wood, for the South Shore extension, central area and much else. Indeed, Mawson did produce plans for the re-building of a great part of Blackpool but his death robbed us of the realisation of that vision. Of his love affair with the resort he tells a fascinating story:

*"Shortly after receiving my first commission for Blackpool, I was staying at Royton Cottage, where I met an old gentleman -who was a typical Lancashire businessman, a keen observer and a philosopher in his way. "I am glad to see you are going to make Blackpool beautiful, Mr Mawson, for it really deserves*

it. Do you know," he continued, "If it wasn't for Blackpool there'd be a revolution in Lancashire?"

"Whatever do you mean?" I asked in some alarm.

"I mean what I say, for down there," pointing towards the industrial towns, half-enveloped in smoke, which lay within the panoramic view, "men stick it as long as they can, and once a year they must either burst out or go to Blackpool; and there they go, and after a fortnight they come back quietened down and ready for work again. Blackpool stands between us and revolution. May it long continue as the protector of social order."

## Good Times, Bad Times

Naturally, the work of designing and redesigning Blackpool did not always go smoothly. These were the years leading up to the Depression and lean times were again on the horizon, with massive unemployment. Sometimes there was open hostility to the arrival in town of 'off-comers,' as in January, 1930, when 200 miners drafted into Blackpool under Government training scheme, got a shock while working on the new aerodrome being built at Stanley Park. They found themselves being chased by angry local unemployed men who resented their importation. But Blackpool was fortunate in that – its civic leaders and officers maintained faith in the future and plans continued apace. In May, 1934, for instance, among schemes afoot were extension of the five-mile Promenade with rock walks and gardens, at a cost of £35,000; a new ballroom floor at the Tower; covered baths and sun

*Taking baby on holiday was never easy. Thank goodness for Ovaltine Rusks! (Daily Sketch, September 21, 1937)*

lounge on the North Promenade, about £100,000; and the rebuilding of Stanley Terrace.

A little less than a year later, perhaps with an eye to customers drifting away from hotels and guesthouses, the Council in March, 1935, passed a resolution expressing alarm at the rapid growth of, and lack of control over, holiday camps, and urging the Government to promote legislation to enable local authorities to make regulations 'with regard to the establishment, registration, regulation and good government of holiday camps.' Anyway, despite the sombre news coming from the Continent, the rise of the Nazis and Fascism in Germany and Italy, Blackpool went on its way in buoyant form. The *Preston Guardian*, July 27, 1935, reported: 'At a private meeting on Wednesday, Blackpool Town Council decided to push forward with schemes which would ultimately cost nearly £1,000,000. The schemes include: A new Town Hall to cost £400,000; an underground garage and conference hall to cost over £100,000; and a health centre, the cost of which has not yet been finally estimated. All these buildings will be erected on the Pembroke Estate, North Shore, land which was purchased recently from a London syndicate for £55,000. The whole scheme is to provide Blackpool with one

of the finest civic centres in the country. It is hoped to start work on the first part of the scheme, the erection of the new Torn Hall, within the next two years. The schemes will find work for hundreds of local men.'

That work was desperately needed. Blackpool saw real poverty in these days. The cold statistics of municipal year books do not reveal that for many the early and mid-Thirties were a time of struggle and hardship, scrimping and saving, soup kitchens and distress funds. The cost to Blackpool of poor relief increased by more than £16,000 a year between 1930 and 1933. There were many cases of petty theft such as coal from the railway sidings, and much sympathy for the defendants. Often the resort's magistrates found ways of minimising penalties, for much of this petty crime was borne of poverty, not criminality.

However, the town never allowed itself to be bowed by these times, largely as the result of the strength of character and sheer force of personality of its councillors and officers. In 1938, for example, James Drake became Borough Surveyor, at the age of only 31, a man of exceptional ability whose contribution to Blackpool was held back by the outbreak of the Second World War, for after the war he was appointed County Surveyor

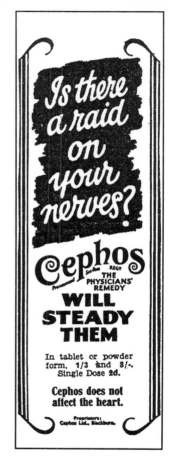

*Your nerves took a real battering with the threat of air raids. But Blackburn-manufactured Cephoss (pronounced 'See-Foss') would do the trick. Preston Guardian, September 30, 1939.*

*Why not cycle to Blackpool on a Hercules bike, for 'two bob' a week? (News of The World, February 24, 1935.)*

and Bridgemaster, a post he held with increasing distinction until 1972. He was certainly Blackpool's loss, for James Drake, later Sir James, is widely regarded as being virtually the architect of the County's post-war roads system. When he was at Blackpool he proposed a motorway ring road for the resort – a motorway was built in 1975.

## War-time Blackpool

The outbreak of the war saw difficult years ahead for Blackpool. True, the problem of unemployment was reduced through conscription but many big schemes for the resort succumbed to war-time restrictions on spending and other austerity measures, including a planned rebuilding of the Central Railway Station in the very first year of the war. Every facet of town life was invaded by the war. At its start 37,500 evacuees and civil servants came to Blackpool. Although after the initial scare many returned home within a few months, the military presence remained huge. No fewer than 769,673 airmen received their initial training at the Winter Gardens during the war. The presence of these was an enormous boost to all the resort's entertainment houses, providing a virtually captive audience, so business at theatres and cinemas boomed and the townspeople got on with life despite the strictures of the Blackout and rationing.

The requirements of war-time production led to Wellington bombers being assembled in a new Vickers-Armstrong factory at Squires Gate, later used to make pre-fabricated houses and Hunter Jets, and given over to industrial usage after the war. It was this use of Squires Gate in the War that led to it becoming Blackpool Airport. The aerodrome at Stanley Park had more or less ceased in 1939.

The Council eventually bought Squires Gate in 1962 and the Airport is now one of the most important facilities in the resort. There were dreams even during the war for Blackpool to play an important part in post-war aviation, including the construction of a four-mile lagoon for seaplanes. Plans for that were produced in 1944 along with a scheme for an international terminal at Blackpool, but the austerity of the 1950s meant that it all sank. Interestingly, what had been the former Municipal Aerodrome east of Stanley Park is now the home of the Zoo.

After the war, Blackpool plunged immediately into recovery, not least in the field of housing. A five-year building programme was drawn up so that by 1950 the Corporation would spend over £5,171,000 on housing. They planned to

build nearly 2,500 houses, with an additional 400 or so by private enterprise, to house about 11,500. Post-war Britain was a pretty dull place. Rationing hung on for years, the clamp on local government spending was all-enveloping, but Blackpool did continue to grow. For instance, in 1955 the boundaries of the borough were extended to include a small part of

*Blackpool sun, salt and breezes might not have been kind to your complexion. Could Icilma Vanishing Cream be the answer? (Daily Sketch, September 21, 1937)*

the Urban district of Poulton-le-Fylde. But the war babies were growing up, their parents had had enough of Austerity and the dead hand of bureaucracy, and by the later years of the decade the shackles were thrown off as the 'Swinging Sixties' arrived.

## In the Swing

It was a taste of things to come when the *Lancashire Evening Post* reported in March, 1959, that there were more disturbances in Blackpool from handclapping teenagers after the showing of the Bill Haley film 'Rock Around the Clock', which some towns had banned. And the times themselves were of a kind of brittle uncertainty, for great redevelopment was beginning to take place in the resort, including in the Bonny Street area, where cottages which had been built by the original fisherfolk of 'Black Pool' came tumbling down.

But in the Sixties Blackpool really did swing, for this was the era of 'pop' and coffee bars, sharp dressing, new literature, live shows, and Blackpool had the lot. Commercial television was not yet succeeding in drawing away actors and pop stars in their entirety, so there was an unbroken procession of big names performing in the resort. The decade from the mid-Fifties was a golden age for live seaside entertainment. In 1960,

among entertainers appearing at Blackpool were Tommy Steele, Harry Secombe, George Formby, Bruce Forsythe, Adam Faith, Eddie Calvert, Dana, Bob Monkhouse, Alma Cogan, Ruby Murray and Emil Ford. With this confidence in the future of the resort came great schemes and new building. At the end of the 1960s municipal and private building was on a giant scale.

Although nationally the economic state of the country was of cut-backs and financial stringency, Blackpool Corporation planned to spend more than £3 million on projects to improve the resort's image and keep in line with modern trends. The biggest scheme was the new Law Courts building, to cost £750,000 and providing a new County Court, Magistrates Court and offices and parking accommodation for nearly 400 cars.

At Bispham, work had started on a £2 million Technical College and School of Art, and the six-storey hotel and catering department costing £673,000 was due to be opened in September of that year. Ministerial approval had also been received for a £323,000 sixth form college to be built at Highfurlong. A new Talbot Hotel was to receive its first visitors and a 150-acre park was to be developed to serve the Northern end of Blackpool which also hoped to become the third international airport for the North of England. Not all the schemes and dreams came to fruition, of course, but their scale was a yardstick of Blackpool's attitude to the future.

## Pace of Change

The period from the 1970s to date has been one of constant change. In 1974 came the upheavals caused by local government reorganisation, which redrew the map of Lancashire and created the present structure. Two years later much of the old Golden Mile fell to the demolition workers, to make way for a new Golden Mile. Some notion of the pace of change can be gleaned from the first couple of months of 1978, when among schemes under way were the Albert Road car park (770 parking spaces); work progressing on the massive multi-million pound Hounds Hill shopping complex in the town centre; great-progress being made with Coral Island, replacing the old Central Station, which had closed in the 1960s; new buildings going up on what had been the site of Ripley's Odditorium, reference to which is made elsewhere. And what may be described as 'ordinary' buildings vanished by the score, although some of those buildings were a good deal more interesting than many

thought. For instance, the old Fylde Water Board head-quarters in Sefton Street, the place to where many thousands of water rates from all over the Fylde were processed, was demolished in 1975. The building had been used by the water board since 1896 until offices were transferred to the North West Water Authority's premises in Stanley Street, Preston. Antique oak panelling inside the building was sold to California. The Sefton Street area was being redeveloped and the rubble for the building was taken for storage near Inskip to be used in road laying.

That pace of change has continued to the present. The Council has been faced with some complex problems. The 1981 Census revealed that Blackpool's population had declined by about 4,000 to about 146,000 and that about one-quarter of that total (37,539) were pensioners. Blackpool was not alone in this of course. The Census showed that this was the position more or less across the Fylde, many elderly people being attracted to the area as one in which to retire. The figure for Blackpool was 25.8%, that for Fylde 24.9% and for Wyre 23.9%. Over at Lancaster it was 24.1%. The last few years have seen old-established buildings fall or close but Blackpool should be praised for its often successful attempts to save some 'little' features of its past as well as important big ones. Such was the case with a plaque of Blackpool's first coat-of-arms, which became a feature near the Pleasure Park's elevated causeway. This was rescued from former municipal buildings at the corner of Sefton Street and Water Street, now part of the Hounds Hill complex. The building dated from 1910 and the opinion of Sir Harold Grime expressed when he unveiled the crest in its new home was shared by many. 'I hope this relic of the past may long survive and this ultra-modern wonderland which gives so much pleasure to so many millions of people'. In 1984 the North Shore boating pool was completely reworked and at the other end of town the Sandcastle was built on the site of the old South Shore Baths. There were some regrettable losses of architectural features, including The Three Graces, which were prominent on the corner of Church Street and Temple Street. The mid-19th century building's reliefs, by artist Samuel Wood, had been a link with the days when what had become a pizza parlour had been the Temple of Art, so the Italianate Faith, Love and Charity finally met their demise.

The loss of The Three Graces was sad but it has not been all bad news. The Blackpool and Fylde Historical Society are very active in identifying historical features that should be preserved, applying for listing where appropriate, and on occasions individual enterprise has saved features. When the big Co-op building, containing the old Jubilee Theatre, closed in the town centre, Art Deco figures from the ceiling were saved in 1988 by Cyril Critchlow, a local historian. The building dated from 1938. It staged many leading amateur and professional shows and at one period was the home of the 'Blackpool Night' radio shows. However, eventually the Jubilee Theatre could not pay its way and in 1969 was closed and converted into offices. In 1988 the end came with demolition.

In 1986, in one of the resort's bigger property transactions that year, the West Lancs Evening Gazette bought the former Connect offices in Preston New Road to turn them into the paper's headquarters the following year. The company sold its head office in Victoria Street as part of a £13 million-plus deal, which included the sale of the Fishergate, Preston, premises of the *Lancashire Evening Post* which was to move to custom-built headquarters at Fulwood, Preston. And the last few years have been of commercial faith in the future. Welcome investment came from such organisations as Lancashire Enterprises Ltd. A good example of their involvement was the Sycamore Trading Estate at Squires Gate, where Lancashire Enterprises put in a £1 million investment in 1987 when they bought the 13-acre estate. As LEL chairman Jim Mason said at the time: 'The estate is one of the most important developments in Blackpool and we regard it as vital to the recovery of Lancashire industry that the right premises are available in the right location at the right price.' That, of course, is a reminder for visitors that Blackpool is not only about Tower World, the Golden Mile, et al, but also about commerce and industry little to do with holidaymakers, entertainment or tourism.

Much work has taken place along the Promenade with the strengthening of the sea defences, some of which date to the 1890s and many from the 1930s, and which had taken a fair old battering down the years. The work has been of an extremely high standard and the contracts completed on time – the latter a notable fact in itself, perhaps. For example, the £3 million sea front at North Shore was completed about a month early in 1982, the development being commemorated by a plaque set in the Promenade wall stating simply: 'Blackpool Borough Council: Coast Protection Scheme. Cocker Square to Gynn Square. The Worshipful the Mayor of

Blackpool (Councillor Tom Percival, J.P.) declared these works to be completed November 1982.' If memory serves, some rather natty blue curtains covered the plaque until the opening ceremony. And very recent years have seen the opening of such establishments as the Sea Life Centre, which has quickly established itself as a major attraction. It opened in 1990 and the public are particularly fascinated by the sharks. The Sea Life Centre certainly knocks many similarly named attractions in other resorts into a cocked hat.

Even the Victoria Hospital, originally a rather grim 19th century building, has seen great expansion over the past decade or so. About £5 million was spent in the mid-1980s in a continuous policy of upgrading and expansion, with the building of new wings meaning the availability of scores more new beds, bringing total capacity to nearly 1,000 beds and the Victoria being the largest general hospital in the North West outside Manchester. The hospital is an old friend of the resort and of course there are many who have reason to be thankful for its existence. Perhaps an up-to-date history should be written of this place (if one has not already), for there have been some notable incidents associated with it. One of the more amusing is that when it was extended in

1904, the hospital nearly created some of its own customers. A platform built for the official opening ceremony of a new ward collapsed and 'threw a large number of men, women and children to the ground.' Fortunately, none was injured – but the incident hardly added to the dignity of the occasion!

What of the future? An inkling may be gained from a *Daily Telegraph* report of June 1, 1990:

'Although only 10,000 Arabs visited the resort last year, out of a total of 400,000 foreigners, their profile is always high.

'Some arrive in private jets and drive Cadillacs and Rolls-Royces shipped from the Middle East. Others, among them Middle East royalty, are happy to pay £2,000 a month to rent houses.

'Mr. Hall (John Hall, Director of Tourism), said: "The typical Arab visitor is a middle-class professional, travelling in a party of about 15. We also get a few sheikhs."

'The resort's proximity to the British Aerospace factory at Warton first persuaded Arabs to tread the Golden Mile. Sent to Lancashire by their countries' air forces, many fell in love with Blackpool and, in particular, the rides, shows and amusements of its Pleasure Beach. When they had a family holiday, they chose Blackpool as their destination.

'They don't bother with the sands – they just love the Pleasure Beach," said Mr. Hall. "It's the largest amusement park in Europe and they have nothing remotely like it at home. It's that more than anything else that draws them here."'

Well, Arab sheikhs are all very well, and most welcome they are, but it will be by maintaining its original philosophy of being a family resort for all the world that will see Blackpool prosper into the 21st century.

# 2

# Past Glories, future prospects

## Fire!

Firefighters have dealt with some spectacular incidents in recent years, probably the biggest being the Pleasure Beach Fun House blaze, but others have been notable. A potential disaster was averted in 1988 when a blaze occurred in the 16-storey Ashworth Court block of flats in Healey Street. Fumes spread through the whole of the building and firemen were in action on all floors. Gas from broken pipes ignited and the situation was a potential fireball. Three years earlier fire broke out in the North Pier Theatre. The pier was probably saved by the quick thinking of singer Vince Hill and pier manager Philip Lockwood who, along with others, fought the flames with an emergency hose until the fire brigade arrived. This blaze was an example of some of the unusual problems faced by Blackpool's fire fighters. The fire was in the wooden floor of the theatre and the tide was in, so the firemen had difficulty in reaching it. The fire engines were too heavy to take safely on to the pier. Resort lifeboatmen took a hose out to attack the blaze from beneath. The cause of the potential destruction of the pier? Almost certainly a cigarette end.

But it is the big fires of yester-year that Blackpudlians will talk of, such as in January, 1932, when the resort's biggest store, R.H.O. Hills, was destroyed. Not only did the fire brigade have the blaze to contend with, but a 50 mph gale which fanned the flames and swept the water from their jets away from the blaze. The problem was solved by directing the hoses on to the Tower framework so that the water was carried on to the blazing building and all the customers and staff were safely evacuated. Unfortunately, this was not the case four years later, in October, 1936, when a fireman paid the supreme sacrifice. That was on October 7, the day Boots burnt down.

The fire spread very quickly. It broke out in photographic materials in the basement and spread rapidly to become a huge blaze within West Street, Market Street, Corporation Street and the Town Hall. A leading drapery store – Riley's – was destroyed and so were the borough surveyor's offices and local health in-

*The wonderfully ornate Tower Ballroom prior to the fire that ripped through it in 1956.*

surance offices. Tragically for historians, many thousands of plans going back over four decades of Blackpool history were burnt. But the real tragedy of the blaze was the death of a 25-year-old fireman, Raymond Laycock, who was buried beneath tons of rubble in the basement. He was trapped there for 27 hours and seasoned firemen were in tears as they fought desperately to get him out. When his lifeless body was retrieved, it was one of the most emotional episodes in the history of the resort's fire brigade. Thousands of spectators had gathered – as always – to witness the blaze and they remained virtually silent as the limp body was brought out of the debris. Most poignant was that Raymond Laycock had been married only 13 days. His funeral was held at St. John's Parish Church, where he had married Dorothy.

That the town is a major tourist centre probably makes the chance of fire all the greater, and down the years there have been many at holidaymakers' venues.

The Pleasure Beach has been a victim several times. The famous Luna Park was destroyed in 1937 and the following year saw the ornate Pavilion of the North Pier go up in flames. There had previously been a big fire in 1921. In 1939 the Pleasure Beach's Indian Theatre was totally destroyed and, in the same year, one of Blackpool's best-known cinemas, the Imperial, on Dickson Road, became a mass of flames. The 1950s and 1960s saw several major incidents. A most heart-rending fire came in 1956 when the beautiful Tower Ballroom was reduced to twisted fragments. Another leading cinema, the Princess, on North Promenade, was gutted in 1963 and the following year the South Pier's Rainbow Theatre was very seriously damaged. In 1967 R.H.O. Hills, which had blazed in 1932, was again the scene of a disastrous blaze.

In Blackpool's early days – the first fire station was in 1878 where the Hounds Hill complex now is – the fire brigade and police were a combined force, a situation that lasted until the mid-1930s. For most of the brigade's life its headquarters was in Albert Road, these premises seeing the first horse-drawn fire engines being replaced by motorised vehicles which today look quite outlandish, right up to the sophisticated machines of modern times. In the mid-1980s, the fire headquarters was moved to a site off North Park Drive and Forest Gate but the proud traditions and history of the brigade remain intact and the fire fighters go on demonstrating their ability to deal with some of the most serious outbreaks in the country.

Fire has robbed the resort of historical buildings including, in 1989, its oldest. This followed a blaze at Continental Bedding, Church Street, a building that had previously been a market and at one time Raikes Smithy – which had origins three centuries ago. Coincidentally, at the same time, as was pointed out by the sharp-eyed Blackpool and Fylde Historical Society, demolition was taking place of part of the resort's first public building, the Little Vic pub, dating to the 1830s, on the Victoria Promenade, much of the site being occupied later by the Majestic Restaurant. The Continental Bedding fire was among the biggest in recent years. It took place on Christmas Day and totally gutted the old building and the shell had to be demolished.

However, the most memorable fire was undoubtedly that in December, 1991, in which the Fun House of the Pleasure Beach was destroyed. Flames leapt 100 feet high and the Art Deco building, dating to 1936, was totally destroyed. Fortunately, the scores of fire fighters were able to save the rest of the

Pleasure Beach and the reaction of Geoffrey Thompson, its boss, was to plan to replace with the biggest ride in the world. Typical of the spirit of Blackpool.

Lost in the blaze was the body of the famous 'Laughing Man' which had been for so long at the entrance to the Pleasure Beach – but not his head, which was saved because it was being repaired in workshops elsewhere. A nationwide search was made for a new body and the 'Laughing Man' made his return.

*A rare and regrettably fuzzy picture from when there was a great fire at the North Pier on September 11, 1921.*

## Schools close their gates

Fire has robbed the town of well-known buildings, but most come and go in the course of the constant development and redevelopment that takes place in any large town. In Blackpool this has applied particularly to some of the old schools, which have come down left, right and centre. Among them was, in 1986, what had been the widely known Collegiate School for Girls, which went under a number of names since its start in 1928. Collegiate, with its bell tower, wide sweep of steps leading to an impressive pillared portico, was a notable building, but down it came and now houses occupy the area, which also includes what had once been St. Joseph's Boys' College, Newton Drive, which up to 1968 had a boarding section. St. Joseph's College was demolished in 1984.

Of school closures there have been many. Terra Nova, one of the resort's oldest private schools, dating to the last year of the First World War, closed in 1985. It had a particular reputation for music.

Its early premises included a church hall on Whitegate Drive but it spent most of its life in a spacious house in Hornby Road. Other schools continue, such as Elmslie, in Whitegate Drive. Elmslie started as Ellerslie in Mere Road in 1918 and celebrated its jubilee in July, 1988, at the same time as it opened a £200,000 sixth form centre. That new block stands on the site of former old wooden classrooms and a · pleasing aspect of the extension was that one of the school's original pupils, Mrs. Laura Stafford, came back to start the demolition procedure by the use of a sizeable sledge hammer. Elmslie's founder was a far-seeing educationist, Miss Elizabeth Brodie, who had originally been at the Terra Nova School. The Elmslie uniform of purple and gold is said to derive from Elizabeth Brodie seeing a mass of crocuses when the school moved to Whitegate Drive: an entirely believable story, for she was a great lover of flowers. The name of the premises in Whitegate Drive was The Elms – thus the change of name of the school. Twenty-three years later the school came under the wing of the Blackburn Diocesan Board. This school has always had a strong sense of history

and, in the foundations of a new infant block a few years ago, buried a time capsule containing information about Elmslie and life and times generally – including what was 'top of the pops' at the time. It should be very entertaining for future local historians.

In 1986 the well-known Arnold School took over the former Grundy House Museum, which had closed through lack of funds in 1984. The museum was set up following the death in 1949 of Blackpool arts patron Sir Cuthbert Grundy. To help pay for the Grundy building, Arnold sold their former Junior School in Horncliffe Road, which gave way to housing. In 1987 the Hawes Side School in Marton celebrated its 50th anniversary as one of the resort's older primary schools. In 1983 Highfield High School – which for many years had a head by the delightful name of Miss Dora Bloomer -celebrated its 50th anniversary. Tears were shed in 1978 when the old Talbot Road Sacred Heart Roman Catholic Junior School was closed, but the fact is that it had been short of pupils for many years, and it found a much more useful role in the Christian centre it became in 1989 with contributions from many denominations an excellent example of an old building finding an important new role in the community.

Perhaps the outstanding success story of the century has been the Blackpool and Fylde College, which was founded in 1937 as a Technical College – the 'Tech' – and has gone on to become one of the most important educational centres in the country, including its very influential Hotel and Food Studies Department, which has achieved a world-wide reputation. Pleasingly, part of this is still based at Courtfield, a large 1890 house in Hornby Road, which was leased to the old Blackpool Corporation in 1944 as a centre for training for the hotel and catering industry. The house was built and owned by brewer Alderman Robert Mather, Blackpool Freeman and 12th Mayor of the resort. In 1993, the college was incorporated with independent status and it has been a story of expansion ever since the early days in 1937 when evening classes started in Palatine Road. In its first months there were fewer than 20 full-time students. Now there are thousands.

## Churches

The process of change has also been very evident in the church life of the resort, with some old friends leaving the scene, but also new ones arriving. The mid-1980s saw the demolition of the 1910 New Jerusalem Church and hall in Reads Avenue in the centre of Blackpool to be replaced by a new church and hall and housing. Some might argue that the loss of these old buildings is regrettable, and certainly in some cases that is true, but many old buildings have been attacked by enemies such as rot -as was the case with the old New Jerusalem – and repair bills become prohibitive. Other churches have fallen victim to shifting populations, a new area becoming more popular than the previous area, or the demolition of buildings around, leading to declining numbers. Such was the case in the late 1980s with the former Christian Science Church in Whitegate Drive, opened in 1929, which became too expensive for its declining congregation to support.

In some cases, congregations have transferred their worship to church halls when the main church has been disposed of, or adapted the churches to broader uses. Christ Church, one of the better-known churches in the resort, did this in the late 1970s when it was decided to hold all church activities in the church, including meetings of the Sunday School and other parish organisations, instead of in the Christ Church Memorial Hall. This 1860s church had been hit by rot and damp.

The rebuilding of churches is nothing new, of course, for if we go back to the

New Jerusalem Church already mentioned, its first meetings were held in various church halls, then a church was built in Stanley Road, then the 1910 church in Reads Avenue and finally the new church (1986) in Reads Avenue. A rather similar story could be written of the old Victoria Street Congregational Church. That church was originally Newton Drive Methodist Church, rededicated in the new name in 1968, and in 1989 the congregation moved to St. Kentigern's RC Church, the Victoria Street Church being absorbed into the massive new Hounds Hill complex. A new church was then built in Newton Drive – an excellent example of how church buildings start, adapt, close and are re-born. It is sad when buildings are lost. The Whitegate Drive Christian Science Church – more properly First Church of Christ Scientist – which went in 1987, will be remembered by many as having had a particularly distinctive domed roof and impressive portico entrance. Designed by a local architect, Halstead Best, it was built in 1929 and was based on a Massachusetts memorial to the founder of the movement. This building was so distinctive that perhaps it should have been saved, but it was big, the congregation small and consequently finance in short supply.

Of course, it is not always easy to make changes. Many in Blackpool remember that proposed changes to St. John's Parish Church went all the way to a Consistory Court in 1986, the first in the town for about half a century, presided over by Judge Quentin Edwards, Chancellor of the Diocese.

God and Mammon very much went hand in hand in the early days of Blackpool. In the days of the worst vulgarities and excesses of the Golden Mile there was, perhaps not surprisingly, an ever-increasing need for more churches, though many go back to before even those days. For instance, Bethesda Church can trace its roots to meetings held in the kitchen of a private house in the first decade of the 19th century. Other venues were used until the building of a 'proper' chapel in 1825 in Bonny's Lane and this was followed by another in Bethesda Square until it was demolished in the 1970s, when the congregation moved to the Grasmere Road Methodist Church. I've chosen this as an example because that 1825 chapel was the first Nonconformist chapel in Blackpool and was a sign of things to come, for the Nonconformists have been very strong in the resort.

Some churches have the most surprising beginnings. The magnificent Sacred Heart RC Church in Talbot Road – a church of real beauty and dignity – can trace its roots to 1855 when the Rev. George Bampton celebrated, in a vault of the Railway Hotel, the first public Mass in the resort since the Reformation. Whether the congregation was surrounded by beer barrels and casks of spirits I do not know. Two years later a church was opened and this was greatly enlarged in 1894 and a major programme of restoration work started before the First World War. From this church have sprung all the other RC churches in Blackpool. A magnificent building, a strong congregation and a favourite with holidaymakers and those who attend conferences in the resort. The church was designed by Edwin Pugin, a member of the famous family.

Another well-known Roman Catholic church is surprisingly young, for the magnificent Church of Our Lady of Lourdes dates only from 1957, its foundation stone having been laid on September 8, 1955, the feast of the Virgin Mary's birthday. The church was built as a thanksgiving for Blackpool having been relatively unscathed during the Second World War. One fascinating story about this beautiful place is that when early photographs of it were published, some people interpreted a cloud formation above the church as showing a representation of the face of Jesus. The Church of Our Lady of Lourdes was the result of the inspiration of an outstanding Bishop of Lancaster, Thomas Flynn, more details of whom will be found in 'Reflections on Lancaster.'

It is said elsewhere that the 1920s were the hey-day of the Golden Mile and the same can be said of church building, some of the best-known in the resort dating to these years, for instance St. Stephen-on-the-Cliffs, North Shore, and St. Mark's, Layton, both Anglican, both 1927. And another particularly wellgown Baptist church also dates from this year, that in Whitegate Drive, a church that could trace its roots to 1910. Having mentioned St. Stephen-on-the-Cliffs, it is worth recalling that this splendid church would not exist but for the exertions of its first vicar, the splendidly named Canon Frank Bertram Freshwater. The good canon made the forming of the parish of St. Stephen's a personal crusade, constantly pushing the church authorities into backing his plans. When the church did open he had every reason to be proud. The Bishop of Blackburn consecrated St. Stephen's, the first in the new diocese of Blackburn.

Sometimes when building work has taken place around churches, interesting discoveries about the town have been-made. Many years ago, when workers were digging new drains alongside St.

John's Church in New Street, they un-earthed an unmarked coffin. It was thought that the coffin had lain in consecrated ground, the boundary of which had become unclear down the years. Interestingly, coffins from St. John's graveyard were reinterred in Layton Cemetery in 1939 when the public footpath and gardens were being laid out. Over the years Tarmac and paving stones cover much and it is not surprising that, if there are few exact and easily accessible ancient records, memory fades and old boundaries become vague. The 1980s saw a great restoration scheme at St. John's which, incidentally, received a very welcome boost in 1987 from Lord Delfont and his First Leisure Corporation in another example of that company's active involvement in all aspects of the resort's life – an affinity with St. John's being especially close because First Leisure's Winter Gardens and Opera House are opposite the church. Half of a £50,000 donation was a personal gift from Lord Delfont and half from the company. At this time the 1878 church faced a number of particular problems including completely re-slating the roof, protection of stained glass, eroded stonework and refurbishment of the organ and bells.

The resort has, in recent years, seen the results of the movement to have very ordinary buildings as churches, or even to meeting in church members' houses. One example was in 1980, when a movement calling itself the Church in Blackpool had been meeting in houses for a decade and then took over an old school at 44 Queen Street, naming it the Forty Four Church Meeting Hall. Two years later they applied to be licensed for marriages.

If there is one thing that Blackpool does not lack, it is sand, 'Seven Golden Miles' of it. This can cause problems with buildings, and churches are no exception. When the wind whips across the Fylde and the sand is in the air, it makes for a superefficient scouring action and churches often find this out to their cost. In the late 1970s Holy Trinity Church on the South Shore faced a hefty repairs bill for repairing the rusted and corroded mountings in the belfry. About 80 years of sand and salt air finally led to the silencing of the bells for several months while the work was carried out. A few years later the town lost one of its landmarks which had finally fallen victim to the Fylde salty rain and wind. This was the spire topping the tower of the United Reformed Church in Warley Road, North Shore.

Recent years have seen the opening of new churches, of course, and their stories are heartening to those who do not believe that the country as a whole is turning from the Church. In 1989 details were published by the Church Commissioners of Blackpool's newest Anglican parish, Hawes Side St. Christopher, under which the Marton church, at that time a daughter church of Holy Trinity, South Shore, was to become a parish in its own right. The old St. Christopher's Church was demolished and in 1991 a new church was opened, services having been held in the church hall while the demolition and building operations were carried out. A great deal of the money for the new church, which cost about £400,000, was raised by local people – a true example of faith in action and practical Christianity.

## Entertainment

Blackpool has features known the world over – the Tower, the Pleasure Beach the piers and the Illuminations. All keep themselves right up to the minute in their facilities and their influence has spread world-wide. In 1993, Illuminations Department features were sold to Jeddah, on the Red Sea – including Larry the Lamb characters! Apparently the Mayor of Jeddah had been on holiday to Blackpool and had liked what he saw. And Blackpool Illuminations are found in other countries, including in Tripoli in the Lebanon, where presumably the notorious Colonel Gaddafi admires them.

As the resort's entertainment industry expanded in the last years of the 19th century, so some of the original venues fell out of fashion. By the turn of the century the originally hugely popular Raikes Hall Gardens, dating to the early 1870s, had fallen on hard times, they closed in 1898 and came up for sale in 1901.

Some idea of the entertainment on offer can be gleaned from the title of one of the 1900 attractions – the Savage South Africa Show. The name Raikes lives on, of course, not least in the Raikes Hall pub. In 1988, when the Raikes Hall was completely refurbished, its function room was adorned with a collection of oil paintings of Blackpool pubs dating back over a century. The original Raikes Hall had not only theatre and gardens but a boating lake and race track.

Budgets in the entertainment world were tight over many periods. In 1901, for instance, although reporting increased business, the directors of the Winter Gardens and Pavilion Company recommended payment of only the same dividend as the previous year, a not very impressive 3% as against the 6%

which went to the shareholders of the Tower Company. And in the same year the directors of the Gigantic Wheel Company reported on the 'adverse circumstances which have operated against the interests of all entertainment prospects during the past season.' Here the dividend was 3% and the capital of the company was reduced.

In the early years, just as with today, fashions in entertainment and recreation waxed and waned, sometimes producing off-beat problems. In 1909 it was reported that there was a roller-skating craze at Blackpool and that the 'well paved promenade',' which had 'a splendid surface,' was 'daily the resort of several hundred skaters, mostly children.' For a few years there was a horse race-course at Squires Gate. The Clifton Park Racecourse opened in 1911, backed by luminaries including Lord Lonsdale, Sir Peter Walker, Bart., and the Squire of Lytham. But the course had a chequered career, never really prospered, and after three years went into the hands of receivers, although it did lurch on with racing until 1915. Then the ground and buildings were taken over by the army as a convalescent and training centre. Eventually the area became Blackpool Airport. Interestingly, the late 1970s saw a revival of interest in having a horse race-course for the resort. In 1978, there

was much talk in the Council of the possibility of a course on land East of East Park Drive, but the sheer cost – up to £3 million, it was claimed – proved intimidating and nothing emerged.

The Opera House is immensely popular. It is a wonderful building and the breadth of variety of its shows breathtaking. Its manager for years was Peter Webster, who kept it at the front line of entertainment. When he retired, his position was taken over by Alan Marsden, who in October, 1982, showed a glimpse of future success in that every ticket was sold for his first Opera House concert, starring the Three Degrees. Around the same time, a new look was embarked on by several other venues, including the Central Pier, where the previous Good Old Days shows were to be replaced with shows with top-line artistes including the likes of Frankie Vaughan, Vince Hill, The Bachelors and Tom O'Connor. An impressive line-up, but impressive line-ups have always been the stock-in-trade of the resort. When the Opera House was chosen in 1955 for the first out-of-London Royal Variety Show, what a show it was! Gracie Fields, George Formby, Eddie Fisher, The Crazy Gang, Arthur Askey, Albert Modley, Charlie Cairoli, Alma Cogan, Jewel and Warriss, Reginald Dixon, Morecambe and Wise, Al Read, Wilfred Pickles, Joan

Regan, The Five Smith Brothers, Geraldo and his Orchestra. Beat that!

The years immediately prior to the Second World War saw much redevelopment of Central Blackpool, including the Opera House. In October, 1938, the then 27-year-old building, without any farewell ceremony, closed its doors after the final performance on a Saturday night and the following Monday morning 60 men marched in with picks and shovels to start demolition. Within a few weeks the old Opera House had totally disappeared, to be replaced in a few months with the new Opera House, complete with a 'super cinema, 100ft stage and seating capacity for 2,800. This was the biggest reconstruction plan in the history of the Winter Gardens Company and it put the resort in the front rank of the theatre world, enabling the staging in their entirety of the biggest of London productions. No theatre in the provinces was to be so big and only two in London would bear comparison – the Palladium and Drury Lane. The cost of the scheme exceeded £100,000. Recent years have seen many wonderful shows at the Opera House, one of the leading productions being 'Cats,' when the whole of the theatre was transformed. The preparations for this show give a pretty good idea of how well Blackpool can rise to the occasion. In the show one of the principal Cats was catapulted up through the stage floor and several feet into the air by means of a specially constructed 'Star Trap' which involved removing the pipes of the theatre's Wurlitzer organ. The orchestra pit disappeared beneath a platform forming an extension to the stage, the walls and ceiling of the theatre were covered with a total of 29 miles of fibre optics and the set ended up looking like a well-organised rubbish dump, exactly what was required. The record-breaking Andrew Lloyd Webber musical was presented by Cameron Mackintosh and the Really Useful Theatre Company in association with Apollo Leisure.

The waxing and waning of public demand and commercial pressures and finance has frequently led to a 'new look' and new organisers for old-established features in the resort's calendar, and sometimes the negotiations can be complex. In 1986 the Miss Blackpool beauty competition, for years a mainstay of the resort, was taken over by First Leisure (although the Council retained the licence and rights to the contest). The change took place following First Leisure negotiating with Eric Morley, of Miss World contest fame, to hold a rival Miss Blackpool UK competition. When the Corporation passed the Miss Blackpool contest to First Leisure, the company undertook to cease with their rival event. Six years earlier, the resort suffered the rare occurrence of losing an attraction to a rival resort. That was the televised final of the Miss UK beauty contest, which went to Brighton. It had been televised from Blackpool for over 20 years. The last Blackpool-elected Miss UK was Carolyn Seaward.

## Battles of the Lights

As mentioned elsewhere, there was intense rivalry for years between Blackpool and Morecambe in the magnificence of their Illuminations, but by 1953 Morecambe had lost the battle. That year the weekly paper at Morecambe, the *Visitor*, had to admit: 'We cannot hold a candle to Blackpool.' Presumably in an effort to engender sufficient jealousy in Morecambe to get them to beef up their own scheme, the editor of the *Visitor* sent a reporter to Blackpool and then published his rather breathless report:

> 'Blackpool's publicity manager, Mr. Harry Porter (late of Morecambe), told me: "There are 300,000 lamps, 75 miles of cable and 50 miles of festoon strips in our Illuminations." I travelled the entire length of the Promenade. It was obvious, even without Mr. Porter's remarks, that Blackpool treat their Illuminations as a business. Their Illuminations Department staff of 160 (including five artists) have really worked their imaginations. Every lamp post is decorated with lights –

> Disney characters, weeping willows, winking bulbs. Colour, movement and ingenuity create a charm and magnetism hard to forget. It makes obvious the reason why Blackpool Lights are preferred by most people. It is this combination of charm and movement. The movement thrills, the charm soothes and provides relief from the excitement of large working tableaux. Most spectacular is a large tableau of a circus over 60 feet long in which every figure moves. The signs of the zodiac wink at you. Large illuminated models of crabs, lobsters, sea-horses and mermaids crowd the Promenade. Model stained glass windows of the first Queen Elizabeth and our present Queen, Duke of Edinburgh, Duke of Cornwall, and Princess Anne with the signatures of the two Queens underneath spring to life piece-by-piece like a giant jig-saw puzzle. Giant models of nursery-rhyme characters loom at you. The variety is unlimited for the entire seven-mile stretch of Promenade. There are many black spots but these are compensated for by the bright original models at the end of them.'

The *Morecambe Visitor* said its report was 'not an advertisement for Blackpool,' but it would be difficult to produce a better one and it remains an excellent description of the Lights of all those years ago.

Four years later, when the United States Ambassador John Hay Whitney, switched on the Illuminations, he told the assembled throng that the display was even brighter than the world-famous 'Great White Way' of Broadway, New York. He said: 'In America, we pride ourselves on the fact that the gayest lights in the world are on Broadway but I am sure that this something that will tell Broadway to fold up.' Later years have seen the Illuminations reach new peaks of excellence while those of other resorts have dimmed and there have been some wonderful personalities to perform the Switch On. In 1983 Doris Speed, the landlady Annie Walker of 'Coronation Street,' was accompanied by many other stars from that programme. In 1986 it was the roly-poly comedian Les Dawson, a few months after the death of his first wife, Meg. (Les himself died in 1993). And muscle was brought in for the 1989 Lights with boxer Frank Bruno in the first Switch On ceremony to be covered live by both television and radio. The fact that there was the mother of all downpours did not help with the technicalities of the proceedings but the event was a knockout success.

Depending on how pedantically one reads local history, the Illuminations started either in 1897 or 1912. In 1897 it is recorded that five illuminated trams moved up and down the Promenade to celebrate Victoria's Jubilee, the idea being borrowed apparently from Berlin's celebrations of the birthday of the Kaiser. By 1912 'decorative lighting' was a feature of Blackpool and that is the year Blackpool regards as being the official start of its Illuminations, the Golden Jubilee having been celebrated in 1982.

The First World War interfered with the growth of the Lights, and then, in 1923, the resort staged an enormous Carnival. The Second World War dimmed the Lights again but 1949 saw their return and the start of the growth into the huge feature they have become. Their importance to the resort is obvious and has been recognised for many years. The *Blackpool Gazette and Herald* reckoned in October, 1934, that when the Lights ceased that year, thrown out of work would be:

❏ 2,000 servants from the staffs of hotels and boarding houses.

❏ 1,000 waitresses and kitchen servants in restaurants and cafes.

❏ 2,000 drivers on motor coach services.

❏ 1,000 people employed in the amusement trade.

In 1978, the Council decided that the Illuminations should shine for eight weeks every year. In the past the display had sometimes been restricted to seven weeks to take account of the variations in the calendar. At the same time the Switch On was fixed for a Thursday night instead of the traditional Friday, to give landladies the opportunity of increased bookings for the first weekend of the Lights.

Pleasure Beach, by Night, Blackpool.

*An excellent series of locally-produced postcards from Allen and Sons, Blackpool.*

ILLUMINATED GONDOLA, BLACKPOOL.          965.

651.     PROMENADE AND CLIFFS, N.S. BLACKPOOL ILLUMINATIONS.

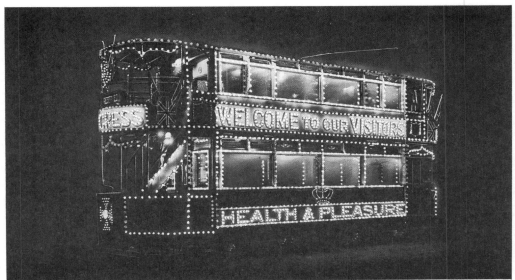

The following year's Lights bore out the wisdom of those decisions for the Lights were described as the most successful ever and it was reckoned that £50 million in trade had been brought into the resort. An estimated eight million visitors made the trip to Blackpool. In 1982 laser lights were introduced, cutting through the night sky with brilliant beams of colour. New features are added to the Illuminations every year and the statistics become ever-more breathtaking. In 1991 there were more than 500 designs and 60 major tableaux, over 120 km of cable and wiring and more than 80 km of festoon strip. That year the Switch On was carried out by radio and television stars Derek ('Morning, morning') Jameson and Judith Chalmers.

There has not always been a celebrity Switch On for the Illuminations and recent years have seen a little re-writing of local history. For years it was thought that the first celebrity was in 1936, when Sir Josiah Stamp did the honours, but then, in 1977, it was found that Lord Derby switched on the Lights in 1934 and, in 1982, it was discovered that a grandmother living in Canada had carried out a Switch On ceremony in 1935 when she was a 15-year-old schoolgirl, Audrey Mosson. Of course the Illuminations cause traffic congestion on a huge scale. It is, after all, the greatest free show on earth, and attempts have been made to deal with the traffic, some more successful than others. In 1979 there was a proposal to seek powers to levy a toll on Illuminations traffic using the Promenade. That was dropped on two main grounds: Parliament is usually against giving local authorities new powers and that the cost of promoting even a relatively uncontroversial Bill could have exceeded £100,000.

## Innovation

The quest for innovation – there must always be something new in Blackpool – has led to the multitude of attractions. An unusual one opened in 1987 was the Wall of Fame at the entrance to the North Pier. Here the handprints in concrete of many stars are on show so you can match your handprints. Every Summer the handprints of more stars are added. Among the first handprints were those of Lord Delfont, then chairman of the First Leisure Corporation, Joe Longthorne, Cannon and Ball, Dana, Roy Walker and Linda Nolan. The Wall is an innovation that may well be unique in this country. The Wall of Fame is, of course, a public attraction.

*Vanished glory from Blackpool's past, the old Palace Theatre, later cinema. The name Harry Lauder occupies a prominent position among the bills for stars appearing and no doubt the audiences rolled in the aisles for such delectations as 'Stop Yer Ticklin' Jock,' and 'I Love a Lassie.' The Scots comedian, born in 1870, who worked first as a mill worker and miner, went on to become Sir Henry Lauder and died in 1950.*

*Below: the ornate interior of the Palace at about the time the novel idea of adding sound to films was coming to fruition.*

What may not be known is that there is in Blackpool a 'floor of fame,' for since the late 1940s, when stars stayed at the guest house of the Roberts family on Norbreck Drive, they left their signatures in wet concrete on the patio. This makes the flags read like a Who's Who of Show Business – Paul Daniels, Barbara Windsor, Michael Barrymore, Edmund Hockridge, Joan Turner, Vince Hill, Sid James, Morecambe and Wise, John Inman, Des O'Connor.

## The Tower

What can be said about the Tower that has not already been said? It has one of the most immediately identifiable silhouettes in the country – even people who haven't been to Blackpool know what the Tower looks like, but the inside has changed dramatically in recent years. In the last few years millions of pounds have been spent in transforming the Tower into Tower World – including the replacement of the original lifts which had been installed in the original structure of 1891. Now it takes only 60 seconds to get to the top – an experience in itself. In 1991 there were already signs of the recession to come so it was an act of commercial courage for First Leisure to embark on the mammoth scheme, probably the biggest 'refit' since the

*Linda Nolan, one of Blackpool's home-grown stars, who became 'Maggie May' of the Central Pier.*

Tower was built. Before Tower World opened in May, 1992, 10,000 children from throughout Britain were taken there by the Variety Club of Great Britain for a giant party to celebrate. They don't do things by halves in Blackpool! 1994 was particularly notable, as plans were made to celebrate the centenary of the Tower and, incidentally, the Grand Theatre.

## Cinemas, Piers and Palaces of Fun

As with most other towns, one feature of life that has become rare in the resort is the cinema. At one time there were many, their names coming down the years as beacons of a past age – Empire, Regent, Imperial, Waterloo, Dominion, Oxford, Coliseum, Tivoli...Most gave way to bingo and retail development and night clubs and even the names seem to belong to an age of different social and political values. Oh well, that's progress, and at least recent trends nationally show that the cinema is regaining lost ground. Perhaps we will witness new cinemas opening in the resort in the next decade – but it is doubtful that they will be as grand as some of their predecessors.

All the Piers suffered considerable damage in the severe storms that battered the North West and much of the rest of Britain in the early months of 1983. The winds of those gales reached 80 mph and more and not surprisingly for Victorian structures the penalty was cracked cast-iron, smashed glass and pulped decking. Similar damage had been caused in storms only five years earlier. But that all the piers have survived to the present day is testimony to the skill and ability of the Victorian builders and engineers. In 1985 a massive face-lift took place on the South Pier, with replacement of the wood including the importation of 40,000 feet of the exotically-named African opepe wood, reported to be so hard that it is impossible to knock nails in it without first drilling holes. The boarding that that wood has formed is expected to last 30 years of pounding from millions of visitors and the salty Blackpool air. Other improvements at the time included a new shopping mall.

In fact, the mid-1980s saw massive investment in all the piers. Later in 1985 a huge refit of the Central Pier theatre took place when the theatre was replaced with Maggie May's show-bar, with seating for 500 at individual tables and waiter service, which has proved to be phenomenally successful. Top of the bill when Maggie May's opened was, of course, home-grown star Linda Nolan as

Busy morning on Victoria Pier, Blackpool

*The old Victoria Pier with its ornate structure that survived fires, floods and powerful tides.*

Maggie May. From being in the original Nolan sisters she has progressed to carve out a top-line individual career. In 1988 the go-ahead came for the transformation of the Central Pier when many of the smaller attractions were done away with, including the well-known circular cinema, and work started on a two-storey amusement arcade with high-level walkway, new adult and children's rides and two-storey circular bar and restaurants. The last of the old-style shows to be held in the Central Pier's old theatre was Mike Donohoe's 'Great Old Days of Music Hall' and when the curtain came down on that it was the closing of an era in Blackpool entertainment – but also the start of an exciting new era of new-style entertainment.

In the same years much work took place to transform the North Pier – the resort's oldest – to give it a Victorian theme.

When the new-look North Pier re-opened it was Blackpool at its best, for there was a parade on the Promenade of

*A rare early view of the Tower Circus, then called "The Tower Menagerie and Monkey House"*

vintage trams carrying guests in Victorian costume – and in the Merrie England bar beer was sold at a penny a pint (alas for only about an hour!). To bring further extravagance to the occasion, Karl Bartoni, mentioned elsewhere in 'Reflections,' upside down and inside a straight jacket, carried out a death-defying stunt in which, with circus artiste Maroia Spencer suspended beneath him by her hair, was hoisted over 80 feet in the air. The rope suspending them was then set alight. In true show business style, the authorities would not let the stunt go ahead until Karl had taken out a £1 million insurance policy. Having successfully carried out their escape, both no doubt needed a drink on the 'new old' North Pier. Special guests at the opening included Blackpool's Mayor, Councillor John Lander, and Deputy Mayor, Councillor Leo Pomfret, with their wives.

The huge Sandcastle complex on the Promenade opened in 1986 and despite chequered financial fortunes, this 'inside seaside' has attracted millions of visitors (it reached its millionth within 15 months). The vast centre, with its glass walls, has been one of the biggest investments in the future of Blackpool and can hold up to 6,000 people at a time with about 1,500 square metres of water available. Truly a modern fun palace it is good, and it should be, for it cost about £16 million to build and equip, a sum that gives some idea of the amount of money that is needed to keep Blackpool as the premier resort. The statistics of the building, as announced at the time of its opening by its joint builders, the Council and Sunley Leisure, are impressive. They include that the four pools contain 300,000 gallons of water and over 2000 tons of steel were used in the construction – not to mention the six and a half miles of beer piping!

Fun palaces there are a-plenty in Blackpool, but for many visitors, the traditional stick of Blackpool rock, excitement of the Pleasure Beach and ride on the trams, are still the essence of the resort. But even something as apparently innocuous as that red-covered, wonderfully crisp and then gooey Blackpool rock (a sure conversation prompter is, just how do they get the letters to go right through the stick?) has come to the attention of the interfer-

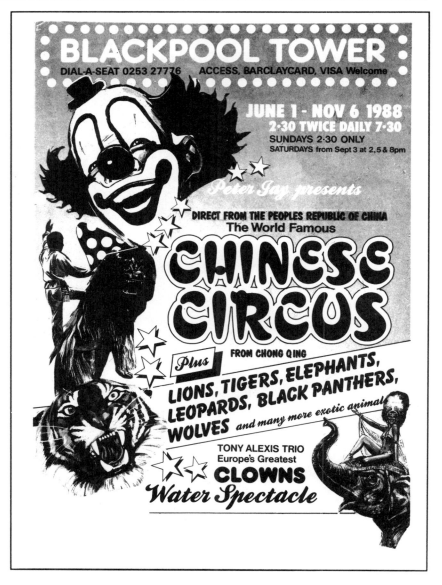

ing bureaucrats, both British and European. Back in 1984 there was a considerable hoo-ha when new trading standard regulations stipulated that to describe rock as 'Blackpool rock' or 'Brighton rock' or 'Morecambe rock' it must have actually been produced in those towns. Blackpool need have no fear. Rock is made in the resort by the ton at such companies as the Fylde Coast Confectionery Company and the Coronation Rock Company Ltd. In 1993 Eurocrats started making disapproving noises about the colourant used to produce that delightful red colour. But the sale of rock has always been a pretty closely watched affair. In December, 1903, the Blackpool Watch Committee decided to ban the sale of rock on the sands the following season. The *Visitor* newspaper in the rival resort of Morecambe rather gloatingly reported of the Blackpool decision: 'This decision of the committee has been come to owing to the abuse of the privilege and the complaints the police have had respecting the methods of some of the sellers.'

The 1970s saw the end of one of Blackpool's more unusual venues on the Golden Mile, Ripley's Odditorium, which advertised itself on a huge sign as a 'Showplace of Oddities, Curiosities and World Wonders.' The closure took place with the redevelopment of the

Golden Mile, so no longer could folk gawp at such novelties as the giant hairy Sasquatch monster, the two feet high Chinese dwarf, the two-headed goat, items used in witchcraft and dozens of other freaks and frighteners which would have been more at home on the Golden Mile of the 1920s and 1930s. Ripley's was Canadian-owned and the only Odditorium in Europe, the others being in Canada and the United States.

New attractions are opening all the time, of course – and sometimes they return after having fallen out of favour originally. Such is the case with the Super Bowl, yet another first Leisure enterprise. Blackpudlians will remember this as originally the Savoy Bowl, born in the ten-pin bowling craze of the 1960s and early 1970s. However, in those days the game was rather heavy and laborious and the Savoy just sort of faded away. Now, with electronic advances, ten-pin bowling is back, the super Bowl replacing the Savoy after 15 years.

Another important addition has been the Sea Life Centre, where the dramatic displays are breathtaking – including the seven feet long sharks. The whole place is an ideal mix of education and entertainment.

Changing times and attitudes led to the Tower losing what had been one of its leading attractions. From 1894 to

1990, the animals of she Tower Circus pulled in the crowds but among those crowds was a substantial number of people who queried the use of animals as entertainment. In the 1980s a strident campaign reached fever-pitch and in 1987 the First Leisure Corporation agreed to the ending of the use of animals in 1990, when the contract with circus proprietor Peter Jay was due to end. The campaign against alleged poor conditions in which the animals were housed, led by Blackpool animal lover Pat Simpson, was vociferous and well-organised and received a huge amount of media coverage. It was destined for success. An astute move was the buying of shares in First Leisure by members, meaning they could get access to Lord Delfont. On the other hand, First Leisure handled the affair with considerable panache and discretion and there seems ample evidence that the public's appetite for the use of animals as entertainment was waning in any event (although the circus, now at South Shore, is very popular), witness the decline, closure and demolition of neighbouring resort Morecambe's Marineland, Europe's first Oceanarium built in the 1960s.

Having decided to get rid of the animals, 1991 saw the new Tower Circus embroiled in a bizarre row dubbed by the Press the 'Werewolf Brothers.' The circus had taken on two Mexican brothers who, because of a rare disease, had face and bodies covered in dark, curly hair. Despite the boys saying they were treated better at Blackpool than in Mexico, and that they were happy with their entertainment role, childcare organisations expressed themselves outraged and the County Council launched an inquiry. The brothers, Larry and Danny Romos-Gomez, were not impressed by claims that they were being used as a freak show, something the circus strenuously denied. The local Press had a field day, of course. The County Council found that the Mexican circus the boys were with had not applied to the local education authority for the brothers to perform and ordered them to be withdrawn from public performance.

# 3

# Blackpool Buildings

## Ups and Downs of The Grand

As with most seaside resorts, buildings come and go in Blackpool at a rapid rate. There is little of permanence apart from a few major exceptions. But when there is something really worth saving, the resort's people are not slow to come forward with their support. In recent years this applied particularly to the fight to save the magnificent Grand Theatre, which celebrated its centenary in 1994. In the 1960s the Grand fell on hard times and as the 1970s dawned the decision was taken to close it. There were plans for major redevelopment of this area and the Grand was to be swallowed up in a welter of new building. But Blackpool has a formidable theatrical lobby which immediately swung into action and great pressure to save the Grand also came from many national show business names who held the resort high in their affections. Peti-

tions flew thick and fast, public meetings were held, a Friends of the Grand organisation was formed, all leading up to the holding of a public inquiry in August, 1973, which ruled in favour of saving the ornate building.

The battle to save the Grand was long, hard, often dispiriting and sometimes acrimonious. Although the decision of the 1973 inquiry stopped the bulldozers, what of the Grand's future use? Owners EMI were keen to use it for bingo and so the Grand would go the way of so many theatres and cinemas in Blackpool and, indeed, the rest of the country. In 1976 they sought planning permission to change the use of the Grand for bingo 'in addition to or as alternative to the existing use.' It was little comfort to the admirers of the theatre as a theatre that at the same time EMI announced they would spend £200,000 to make the Grand 'the most luxurious and the most attractive bingo hall in the United Kingdom,' but would do nothing which would 'permanently inhibit the Grand's use as a theatre.' An EMI official quoted in the *Blackpool Herald* of November 26, 1976, said: 'The theatre will be completely restored to its former glory with the help of a design consultant working together with the Tower Company's architects in a way which we believe will not be incompatible to bingo.' Half a loaf better than none?

The Friends of the Grand supported the bingo use with their long-term ideal in mind. Negotiations with EMI led to the giant company granting the Friends an option over the next 20 years to buy the Grand – if they could raise the money. What the Friends feared, of course, was that the theatre would be left empty with inevitable deterioration, but it must be said that EMI were as good as their word. In May, 1977, EMI were granted a gaming licence for the Grand, prompting the Blackpool Free Church Federal Council to announce that to use the building for bingo would be 'prostitution of a fine building'.

EMI forged ahead with the restoration of the interior, enabling bingo fans to play in a wonderfully ornate and plush venue – gold leaf on the plasterwork on the front of the balconies – and the Friends of the Grand finalised rehearsals for their first show there, Dora Bryan in Noel Coward's 'Fallen Angels.' Under the agreement with the owners, the Friends could use the theatre once a month for fund-raising shows, the rest of the time bingo holding sway. Perhaps it was an omen of good fortune that the site foreman at the Grand was called Bernard Shaw. This year, 1977, saw the Save the Grand campaign really take off,

**GRAND THEATRE, BLACKPOOL**
Monday, April 19th and week, 1982

Newpalm Productions and
Charles Vance Present

# Jennifer Wilson

## Valentine Dyall      ## Mandy Rice Davies

## Margot Thomas

in

# The Hollow
by
# Agatha Christie

with

## Brian Peck

**Dennis Spencer**      **Pat Brackenbury**

**Directed by Charles Vance**

Settings by Newpalm Productions

*From the 1982 programme of Spring attractions at the Grand Theatre.*

with many show business stars lending their support. In October a superb show was put on by Barry Foster (Van der Valk), Isla Blair (When the Boat Comes In) and Tim Brierley (Royal Shakespeare Company), and a few months later, at the end of March, 1978, the King of Mirth himself, Ken Dodd, officially launched the £350,000 appeal to buy the Grand. Almost 1,000 were in the audience of the free show – after the night's bingo.

Although the campaign drew huge support from members of the public and show business names, the Friends knew there was a huge task ahead. The option to buy was at £350,000 or market value, if higher. But the funds did mount up, even if they came in fits and starts, and the community got behind the cause – £1,100 from the staff and pupils of Rossall School, Fleetwood, for instance – and by mid-1978 a healthy £20,000 had been raised. More and more show business stars joined the campaign, among them Dec Cluskey of The Bachelors, Paul Daniels the magician, comedians Joe Church and Billy Dainty, and Coronation street's Violet Carson (Ena Sharples), who were present when an official brochure was launched from the Grand – show after show and event after event saw the funds total creep up and 1980 saw the arrival of some wonderful news,

the reduction of the original asking price of £350,000 to £250,000. Save the Grand funds had now reached the stage where the Blackpool Grand Theatre Trust were able to take possession, and at the end of September the doors of the theatre were ceremoniously opened by Violet Carson. Major contributions had given the campaign a tremendous boost, among them £100,000 from Blackpool Council, £50,000 from the Arts Council, £20,000 from Thwaites Brewery and £10,000 from the County Council. Smaller contributions continued, of course, costing the givers as much in real terms as the large corporate amounts.

The Grand got the Royal seal of approval when in 1981 Prince Charles attended a glittering Royal Gala Variety Show (only the second to be held in the resort, the first having been at the Opera House in 1955). It had already proved its fitness as a theatre for modern times with a series of successful shows, including the D'Oyly Carte Opera Company, an Old Vic production of The Merchant of Venice, The Mating Game with Barbara Windsor, and an amazingly successful Joseph and the Amazing Technicolor Dreamcoat. And despite setbacks and other financial crises the Grand has continued to survive and demonstrate that it is just as necessary to Blackpool as when it opened for the first time on July 23, 1894. The Grand is, indeed, one of the finest buildings in the town. It was designed by one of the country's most famous theatre designers, Frank Matcham, responsible also for the Opera House, and was opened by Thomas Sergenson, one of Blackpool's major theatrical entrepreneurs (see later). An excellent description of the theatre at its opening is to be found in the *Blackpool Gazette and News*, July 24, 1894, part of which is reproduced:

> Blackpool may now justifiably boast that no other watering place in the world offers such facilities for the recreation and enjoyment of its visitors... But it is not very many years since Blackpool was entirely dependent on what may be described as itinerant entertainers for the amusement of its summer visitors... Mr. Thos Sergenson... must be very heartily congratulated upon the enterprise which has its consummation in the New Grand Theatre and Opera House – admitted on all hands to be undoubtedly one of the finest theatres in the provinces.

> Mr. Frank Matcham, the well-known theatrical architect, of 9 Warwick Court, London, was in the first instance given carte blanche, and as a result of his labours there can be no question that the New Grand Theatre is about as near perfection as architectural skill can make it, and well deserves the title of 'Matcham's Masterpiece.'

> The circular entrance at the corner of Church Street is a particularly fine example of stonework, and the dome and minaret cannot fail to attract the attention of all passing by. The entrance hall is prettily finished off with decorative ferneries and rockeries, while a handsome marble staircase leads to the dress circle and boxes, of which there are eight in number...

> The upper circle will easily seat from four hundred to five hundred... The gallery will provide accommodation for at least 1,000, the view from the stage being uninterrupted, so that not far short of 3,000 persons may witness the performance at one time, all seated. (A fuller extract from this fascinating description will be found at the back of 'Reflections' as an appendix).

Sergenson was one of the great figures of Blackpool and without him the resort would have been without a number of important venues. Thomas Sergenson came to Blackpool from Preston in the mid-1870s. His first work was with the public baths of Hygiene Terrace, later to become the site of the Prince of Wales Theatre. The early years of that theatre were of one financial crisis after another. Eventually Sergenson was offered the ailing property – he had become treasurer in 1879 – but he refused to take it over, waiting another year before he got the lease at budget cost. He turned the Prince of Wales into a profit-making venture and, in fact, was so successful that he went on to take over the leases of other venues, such as the Theatre Royal, and ultimately built the first Opera House and the Grand Theatre. A giant from Blackpool's past, he died in Warwickshire in 1926, five years after moving from the resort. The Theatre Royal, incidentally, was in the building which is now bates' Wine Lodge, an historic building for several other reasons, for it was also for a period Blackpool's first public library (1880) and in the late 1850s Blackpool's first Baptists met there. But to return to modern times and the success story of the saving of the Grand. So many helped save the theatre for future generations that it would be invidious, indeed impossible, to name them all. However, when you are in the theatre, look out for a stained glass window to the memory of Marjorie Higham. She became the Grand Theatre Trust's life president. The window was unveiled in 1982 and is inscribed simply: 'This window is dedicated to the memory of Mrs. Marjorie Higham A.L.A.M. (Hons) (Acting). A True Friend of the Grand.'

## Derby Doom

However, not all 'Save' campaigns in Blackpool have been successful. One that failed was that for the 1938-built Derby Baths, an amazing building reflecting the 'modern' architecture of the era, a great square-angled building looking on the outside somehow like a giant Odeon cinema. It attracted hundreds of swimmers a day in its early years and had seating for about 1,200. Its main pool had numerous lanes. The foundation stone was laid by Alderman Jack Quayle, the Mayor, in July, 1938, and building operations took about two years. The Derby Baths were enormously popular and quickly earned a firm niche in the affections of the townspeople and, indeed, folk from miles around, who would make a whole day out of a trip to 'the Derby.'

During the second World War the military seized upon the Derby and the BBC had a broadcasting station deep within its bowels. But besides the wear and tear caused by all those army boots, the war also led to a diminution in

*The Baths, South Shore, Blackpool.*

*An excellent shot of the South Shore Baths from a postcard postmarked September 8, 1935. Rather more prosaic matters were on the mind of the writer, one 'Ruth,' Addressed to a Mrs. Fish of Sandylands, Heysham, Morecambe, the message is: 'Dear Doris, – I forgot to tell you the fish food is in the pantry. Had a good journey down and got fixed up, very comfortable.'*

maintenance of the building and, anyway, life had changed by the end of the war and it probably never regained its original popularity. The concrete and steel buildings of the 1930s became notorious for corrosion problems – this was one of the features that led also to the demolition of the 1935-built Super Swimming Stadium at rival resort Morecambe – and in the 1970s the crisis point was passed.

On one occasion, October, 1978, the *West Lancs Evening Gazette* reported that there had been so few bathers that they were outnumbered by staff. The Derby Baths staggered on through the 1970s and first half of the 1980s, but the second half of the decade saw the Council having to make the final decision. Three options were open to them: Keep the baths going and continue to lose a great deal of money every year, with costly maintenance of an ageing building; privatisation; demolition.

Some of the people of Blackpool rallied to the cause and there were demonstrations and much banner-waving, including children from schools which would lose their swimming facilities, but in February, 1988, the final decision to close was made.

Unfortunately, the Derby Baths issue became the subject of bitter politics and in-fighting on the Council and the undignified wrangling continued for months. But in the end Blackpool had to say goodbye to the old Derby which, when it opened, was described as covering a site of 8,370 square yards and possessing:

❏ Plunge for 1,700.

❏ Tip-up seats for 1,740.

❏ Bathers' sun lounge.

❏ Sun-bathing terrace.

❏ Remedial baths.

❏ Solarium.

❏ Gymnasium.

❏ Learners' bathing pool.

❏ Hairdressing salons.

For some reason, the closure and demolition of Blackpool's other big baths, the Open Air Bath on South Shore, which had been a splendid 1920s building, never engendered the same public interest as the Derby Baths – which is surprising, for the South Shore

emporium had been modelled on no lesser splendour than the Colosseum of Rome. From its opening on June 9, 1923, to its demise in 1983, it was loved by thousands of bathers. As with the Derby Baths, it attracted hundreds at each session. Within six years of opening, four million people had enjoyed the use of its facilities. That popularity continued through the 1930s, 1940s and 1950s, but by the 1960s – the Swinging Sixties – social fashions had changed and attendances fallen away to mere thousands a year.

Plans to roof the pool came to nought and so did many other schemes to use the South Shore Pool area as anything but a pool and in early 1983, the Council 'took the plunge' and decided on demolition. By mid-March virtually all trace of the old South Shore Baths had disappeared. As usual, Blackpool was looking to the future and work had already started on a scheme for a new centre planned to include a swimming pool, entertainment and conference hall, night club and disco, bars, cafes, restaurants and skating facilities. The South Shore Bath, when it opened in 1923 could boast of being the largest open air swimming pool in the world. It became famed as the venue of the old Cotton Queen, Miss Blackpool and Miss UK bathing beauty contests, and was used scores of times for the making of films. It was used prominently in Gracie Fields' 'Sing As We Go,' for instance. Until 1951, the South Shore Bath also played a major role in the Illuminations. But all that has finished now and Blackpool has marched on leaving only the memory of a place that for many represented a golden age in the town's story.

## The Gigantic Wheel

Of all the structures that have graced Blackpool over the years, the Tower remains supreme, of course, but for a relatively short period there was a rival attraction of equally mind-boggling proportions – the Gigantic Wheel. Built in 1896 by the Gigantic Wheel Company, its vital statistics were astounding.

It stood 220 feet high and weighed 1,000 tons and had 30 carriages, each seating

ROUGH SEA, BLACKPOOL.

*From an old colour postcard, showing the Gigantic Wheel and one of the mighty seas Blackpool is famous for.*

*Late 1920s view of the Gigantic Wheel.*

30 people. But the truth is that although it was a marvel to behold – a favourite postcard of the time was a view of the Gigantic wheel with the Tower thrusting up through the middle – the sheer size of the wheel meant that it was painfully slow in revolving. It did not excite

sufficiently enough pleasure-seeking holiday makers to make it pay its way, so that its days were numbered within 30 years.

When it was built, it cost about £50,000. The Winter Gardens company was taken over by the Tower Company in 1928 and almost immediately the shrewd Tower chairman, Sir John Bickerstaffe, announced that the Big Wheel would soon revolve no more. Its dramatic fall in value had already been demonstrated in 1916 when the Winter Gardens had bought the wheel from the Gigantic Wheel Company for a mere £3,913, However, the Gigantic Wheel Company were convinced they had a sure-fire success and cajoled the crowds with the kind of hype that would not shame our modern film industry. In 1905 they put out a brochure claiming that the site between Adelaide Street and Coronation Street – was the area of the greatest monetary circulation and the greatest crowds during the season, with a great majority of the three million people visiting Blackpool each season spending some time in the exhibition grounds or being carried round the Great Wheel. The company claimed that the wheel was: 'A perpetual sky-sign and everlasting attraction, visible from every part of the town and surrounding country. It is the chief topic of conversa-

PLEASURE BEACH, SOUTH SHORE. BLACKPOOL

*A splendid view of the Pleasure Beach from a postcard postmarked July 13, 1925. On the left Noah's Ark and on the right the Helter-Skelter, with numerous attractions in between, including the Scenic Railway. Written to a Mrs. Helm at 12 Chapel Street, Longridge, Nr. Preston, the message reads: 'Dear Grace, Just a line to let you know that we are having a good time. I saw Mr. Cookson this morning, they are all well, the weather is very hot here and we have a full house, always something going on, with best wishes from yours— A.B.*

tion for the last few miles of the journey by the passengers of every train approaching Blackpool.

Like its counterpart the Tower, the Gigantic Wheel tends to bring on a rush of superlatives. During the first two hours of its opening in 1896, no fewer than 4,000 visited it. The carriages were so roomy that when demolition came at the end of 1928 season, they were sold off to become garden sheds, sports pavilions and in one case, to serve as a dormitory for orphans at a house near St Michael's which later became the famous Big Wheel Cafe. Today Blackpool has another Big Wheel, on the Central Pier, but compared with its predecessor it is a mere tiddler at 'only' 180 feet. It went up in 1990, can carry 200 people, and cost in the order of £3.3/4 million. But somehow the new Dutch-built Big Wheel which involved specially strengthening the pier, does not have the romance of the old Gigantic Wheel, and its bucket-like seating bears no comparison.

## The Tower and Pleasure Beach

The Tower and the Pleasure Beach are still the marvels of the resort. The Pleasure Beach really is an extraordinary place with an extraordinary history. A few years ago Blackpool Corporation provided the following impressive statistics for a season: $47^1/_2$ miles of hot dog sausages are consumed; one million ice cream cones are eaten, 20 million rides are taken; 20,000 packets of toilet paper are used, 150,000 refuse bags are used; there are 380,000 metres of electrical cable; 1,000 mop heads are used; 1,600 five-litre cans of paint are used.So it is with little fear of contradiction that the Pleasure Beach boasts of being the oldest and the largest of its kind, with about 150 rides on its 40-plus acres, getting on for 100 years since the first ride, the Hotchkiss Bicycle Railway was introduced.

Today there are over six million visitors a year and it is a slick and complicated operation which has used Satchi's for advertising. Another of the early rides was the delightfully names Sir Hiram Maxim's Captive Flying Machine in 1904.

It all dates to an extraordinary character called W G Bean, a Londoner with pleasure park experience who in 1896 with John W Outhwaite, came to Blackpool with the avowed intention of setting up: "An American-style amusement park, the fundamental principle of which is to make adults feel like children again, and to inspire gaiety of a primarily innocent character'. Their success speaks for itself in today's massive operation which occupies land once lived on by gipsies. The early years were not without their difficulties, however. In March 1907 for instance the Council drew up new conditions for the regulation of what was known then as the Fairground on South Shore one of them being that 'no Gipsy's tent, shed, caravan, or encampment shall be permitted.' Not surprisingly the gipsies took exception. They had lived there for years and they pointed out in no uncertain terms that they had always lived respectably and paid their rates. There was not total support for clearing out the gipsies. One councillor commented that if it were desirable to debar the gipsies, it was equally desirable to exclude 'palmists, phrenologists, clairvoyants and quack doctors.' He said that these people were a nuisance on the sands 'and did a great deal of harm to young girls and feeble-minded women.'

Despite a quite misplaced yearning for 'respectability' by certain kill-joy councillors, the Pleasure Beach prospered

*An early view of the 1904 "Maxim's Captive Flying Machine". The Maxim of this machine was Sir Hiram Maxim, inventor of the Maxim machine-gun; he was born in 1840 and died in 1916.*

and grew. Some of the early rides have lasted into modern times. It is interesting to note that the Sir Hiram Maxim of the Captive Flying Machine was the inventor of the spectacularly successful machine gun and also an aviation experimenter of some note – he died in 1916. New rides came thick and fast. In 1907 the first scenic railway roller-coaster in the country was installed and in the 1920s came the Big Dipper. These were the predecessors of attractions of recent years like the Revolution, a 360 degree looping roller-coaster, and the Space Invader, a roller-coaster in the dark which simulates space travel, and the Avalanche, one of the most 'white knuckle' of 'white knuckle' rides.

The genius who was Bean died in 1929. One of the special aspects of the Pleasure Beach is that, despite being a multi-million pound business, it remains a family company. After Bean died the Pleasure Beach was taken over by Leonard Thompson, Bean's son-in-law, and today it is run by Geoffrey Thomp-

*Symbols of Europe's greatest amusement park.*

son, Leonard's son, the business having grown through the years to operate Pleasure Parks in Morecambe, Southport and the United States as well as Blackpool. Over the past few years the rides have got bigger and more spectacular and the Pleasure Beach has survived a major fire. A huge revamp took place in the late 1980s-early 1990s and to those who have experienced it, the fact that Blackpool Pleasure Beach attracts more visitors in a year than London's Madame Tussaud's comes as no surprise. It is computed that 80 per cent of visitors to Blackpool go to the Pleasure Beach. The entrance is free and you are charged only for the rides you go on – so what are you waiting for?

The Pleasure Beach is a place of astounding statistics, and so is the Tower. It weighs 2,943 tons and it takes nine tons of paint to cover it. Each of the Tower lifts travels about 3,500 miles a year and 10,000 lightbulbs decorate the structure during the Illuminations. The letter box at the top was installed by the Post Office in 1949. The flagpole weighs 30 cwt. About 2,000 ice creams and 6,000 cups of coffee and tea are sold in the Tower buildings each day and the Wurlitzer organ in the Ballroom delivers over 17,700 'numbers' each season. Yes, the Tower is truly one of the wonders of the land, a fitting rival to M. Eiffel's

structure in Paris. In fact, a start was made on building Blackpool's Eiffel less than three years after the French tower had been built and it has from that day been the dominant building in the resort. There is scarcely a topographical book in the country that does not devote considerable space to the technical wizardry and architectural impressiveness of this leviathan. There have been rivals apart from that in Paris but none has lasted in this country. New Brighton tried to outdo Blackpool in 1898, when it opened a 621 ft. tower, and Morecambe at one period had two towers. But Blackpool's is the only one to survive and 1994 was its centenary, for it was officially opened on Whit Monday, 1894. Even today there are towns foolish enough to dream of rivalling Blackpool's 'Stick,' as the maintenance workers, the 'Stickmen,' affectionately call the Tower. Plymouth had such a plan in 1988 for a tower nearly 100 ft. taller than Blackpool's. It has yet to rise.

Even in the heady days of the 1890s, there were those in Blackpool who felt the resort may have gone 'over the top' and John (later Sir John) Bickerstaffe, one of Blackpool's greatest pioneers and the Tower Company's first chairman, must have breathed a huge sigh of relief that visitors flocked to the Tower from day one. Ironically, from the first day it was recognised that poor weather is the Tower's best friend, for it drives visitors under cover – so presumably the Tower management pray for rainy days. The apathy of Southern resorts was Blackpool's gain, for it is said that the actual idea of the Tower was the vision of a London entrepreneur who failed to excite interest 'down South' and so came 'up North,' where his idea found a hearty welcome. There were set-backs, naturally. In 1897, for instance, only three years after the Tower opened, the top caught fire. Fortunately there were few people around, the blaze was kept under control and re-opening took place very soon afterwards.

It may, perhaps, be rather surprising that it was as late as 1935 that the first visitor was killed falling off the Tower. He was a 20-year-old Londoner who committed suicide by throwing himself from 420 ft. up. There had been previous fatalities with workmen but the records are not very clear. During the Second World War the Tower was used as a Radar station and part of the top was removed. After the war the Tower was used in experiments for television reception in the North. An event that is still remembered by many was a great fire in 1956 when the Tower's wonderful Ballroom was reduced to a smouldering ruin. The Tower has always been a

*The masterpiece that is Blackpool Tower, from a postcard postmarked 1962. 'Tower weather' (see text) seems to have been the order of the day, judging from the message on the back of the card: 'Dear Eileen and Gordon, – Spent the afternoon here as it was so wet but it was packed out and we could hardly move. Our fortnight is flying past and it will soon be Saturday.' The card was addressed to Widnes.*

*Scene in the Tower 'Cafe Restaurant' at the turn of the century. Note the crisp linen tablecloths, serviettes and the pot plants.*

*Scene in the Tower 'Cafe Restaurant' at the turn of the century. Note the crisp linen tablecloths, serviettes and the pot plants.*

profitable venture and even the Second World War and days of Austerity afterwards did little to dent shareholders' dividends. For instance, in 1947 the shareholders received a record dividend and bonus from the company – 35 per cent (made up of 20 per cent dividend and the rest bonus). This was an increase of five per cent on the previous year. Net profit (including interest but before taxation) was £297,278, actually a fall on the £320,870 made the previous year.

Apart from the years immediately after it opened, the past two decades have probably been the most exciting in the history of the Tower. A massive change came in late 1980 when the giant Trust House Forte Company – already running the three piers – took over the Tower, Winter Gardens and Golden Mile Amusement Centre in a reported £16 million deal with Thorn-EMI. There was some opposition. Owen Oyston, a leading Blackpool businessman who made his fortune in estate agency, commented:

'This sale must not be allowed to go through. It is a disgrace that important parts of the Blackpool tourist industry, of vital importance to the local economy, should be bought and sold through financial dealings between London-based conglomerates.' (*Lancashire Evening Post*, November 1, 1980). Nevertheless, the deal did go through but three years later the First Leisure Company was formed after buying the whole of Trust House Forte's leisure division for a massive £37.5 million.

Chairman and chief executive of First Leisure was Lord Delfont, a man with a deep knowledge of Blackpool and the North West generally, and he immediately announced plans to spend £1.5 million on the Tower, regarded as being the 'jewel' of the company.

The ensuing years have shown First Leisure to have carried out a first-rate job with Blackpool, in which it has invested on a huge scale. The company was quite explicit about its faith in the resort. Lord Delfont told the *Lancashire Evening Post*, August 6, 1983: 'We plan to re-invest on a major scale because Blackpool leisure is the gem in our business.' Matters were not hindered when the English Tourist Board awarded a £275,000 grant to the Tower, one of the biggest grants they had ever made. Major changes were made with the

Tower's attractions in the Eighties which proved hugely popular, among them Jungle Jim's, a safari-type adventure playground for children; the Dome of Discovery, a celebration of science and technology; the Undersea World, with over 3,000 fish; Memory Lane, tracing the history of the Tower from its beginning to the present; Penny Lane, packed with the latest amusement machines; and the Good Times Emporium, providing family entertainment – all this in a structure now declared a Grade One Listed Building because of its historical and architectural importance. The success of the new attractions was well demonstrated in that in 1984 for the first time most of the Tower was kept open during the Winter. In 1985 the Tower Ballroom's famous Wurlitzer Organ celebrated its 50th anniversary and business kept rolling in for First Leisure. When record profits were announced for 1985 – over £1 million – there was an interesting historical parallel when Lord Delfont announced that the dismal Summer weather had driven people off the beaches to inside attractions. Memories of those first days in the 1890s when the management prayed for 'Tower Weather.'

## Trams and Transport

With its millions of visitors, its commerce and industry, its entertainment palaces and hotels and guesthouses, Blackpool has always had to keep 'on the move' as far as transport is concerned. From the earliest days it was recognised that if Blackpool was to be successful it must have a good transport system, not only for getting to and from the town but within the resort itself. The earliest visitors arrived either by 'Shanks' Pony' or by various horse-carriages, and then came the railway in 1846, the mode of transport that really put Blackpool on the map, and later came the trams, the landaus, the buses, good roads and even an airport. But it is for the trams that Blackpool is known particularly. No holiday or day trip is complete without a ride on the trams and it is not considered that one has seen the Illuminations in their full glory unless viewed from an Illuminations tram. And this form of transport has a

*Transport of yesteryear: a tram passes the Victoria Pier. Note the elegant street lighting.*

Victoria Pier, Blackpool.

*One of Blackpool's modern trams.*

long and honourable history, for the Blackpool trams celebrated their centenary in 1985 and until modern times tram routes spread for miles around the resort.

There was talk for years of getting trams before they finally arrived and many acres of local newsprint were taken up with the minute detail of lengthy and often wearisome debates. Thus we find in the *Blackpool and Fleetwood Gazette News* in 1883 a report that 'Councillor Harrison moved that it is desirable that tramways be laid on the Promenade from North to South Shore.' The good councillor reminded the meeting that this was the third time he had raised the subject and he commented that 'the wear and tear on the roads with the present omnibus traffic is enormous.' Two years later the *Preston Guardian* reported in July: 'During the week several experimental runs have been made on the new electric tramway which is nearing completion. Three of the cars have already arrived, and it only remains for one or two sections of the track to be completed for the trams to start running regularly. The cars have run satisfactorily so far, and it is believed they will prove successful. There have, however, been complaints in the town about the delay in their construction.'

A little later the trams were formally opened and, despite the Mayor, Alderman Cocker, maintaining that they would not last a couple of years, the trams have always been a big earner for the resort, not only in revenue but also in the enormous attraction they are to holidaymakers. The Blackpool Electric Tramway Company and its successors have been a resounding success. In March, 1901, the Council decided to raise the salary of the Tramway Manager to the dizzy heights of £300 – and there was extra incentive. When the profits of the tramways were to reach £15,000, he was to have £350 salary, and £400 when the profits reached £20,000. These early days were of dreams and schemes. Only about a month later in that year the Blackpool, St. Annes and Lytham Tramway Company was reported to have been bought by a syndicate for £110,000, the total capital of the company being £136,868. The syndicate announced that they were going to do away with gas and substitute with

overhead trolley 'wires.' The line was to be extended to Freckleton, where it was to be converted into a light railway which would extend to Preston, connecting that town with Fleetwood. Ah, the stuff of dreams! In November, 1908, the Southport and Lytham Tramroad Company announced that it was to abandon its ambitions to build a tramway across the Ribble from Southport to Lytham and there link up with Blackpool and Lytham Tramways. In reality, the scheme died from lack of enthusiasm – and it proved costly, for about £46,000 had been sunk in preliminary expenses, mostly legal, and that money had to be more or less written off.

*Blackpool and Fleetwood News*, July 3, 1885:

> *At last, Blackpool people have before them some realisation of Mr. Holroyd Smith's scheme for propelling tramways by electricity, which has been under development for many-months past. One of the cars, which are to run along the Promenade when the tramway is completed, was yesterday put upon a short length of line in Princess Street near to the tramway company's depot and during the day a very large number of persons had the satisfaction of seeing it at work. The car at present on view is a most handsome vehicle and does great credit to the company and to the town which has had the enterprise to enter into so novel a method of locomotion. The friction between the rails and the wheels generated a considerable number of sparks but it is understood that the*

*objectionable feature will not be present when the unevenness of the two surfaces have worn away. At several points along the Promenade, the line of rail has not yet been completed but it is expected that two or three weeks will yet elapse before the tramway is in working order throughout.*

Running the tramways has never been an easy task. There was always the perennial problem of cyclists. All cyclists who remember riding on streets with tram-lines will recall the unnerving experience of getting the cycle wheels trapped in the rails. It is an old problem.

At an inspection of the new Marton electric tramway in 1901, cyclists held a demonstration about the half-inch groove in the road. A tram containing an august body of officials and VIPs, including the Mayor of Blackpool and a Board of Trade Inspector, was brought to a halt by aggrieved cyclists who had wedged two cycles in the rails with placards remonstrating 'Remember the lives of cyclists' and 'Suicide made easy.' The officials were not amused. One

THE PLEASURE BEACH, S.S. BLACKPOOL.    H.2086

*A superb view of the Pleasure Park from a postcard postmarked 1940. In the centre, the Fun House so dramatically razed to the ground in a huge blaze in 1991. When this postcard was stamped, the wonderful Art Deco building was only about four years old. The message on the back of the card was, simply, 'Having a good time, – Lois.'*

'cycle was 'thrown to the pavement' and 'a struggle ensued for possession of the other.' But, as stated, the trams were both profitable and popular and statistics from even the early years are impressive. As the country looked towards the first year of the First World War, Blackpool Corporation's trams were prospering. From April 1, 1913, to March 19, 1914, the receipts totalled £83,178 – £12,798 more than in the corresponding period in the previous year. Nearly 124 million passengers were carried, two million more than in the previous period; and the trams ran over 1,048,547 miles, an increase of 35,216 miles. Not surprisingly, the Promenade section was the financially most healthy part of the system. This showed total receipts of £35,458: £5,306 more than the previous period.

As the trams became more and more strongly established, so the system grew. Other towns around set up their own tram systems but those were all eventually absorbed into the Blackpool system. Perhaps chief among these was the Blackpool and Fleetwood Tramroad Company which started operating between Fleetwood and Dickson Road, Blackpool, in 1897. It is reported that the owners of horse-buses demonstrated against the upstart new company. With headquarters at Bispham, just outside the Blackpool Borough boundary, that system ran in its own right but it eventually went the way of other operators and was taken over by Blackpool Corporation at the start of 1920. The trams continue to be a mainstay of Blackpool and great celebrations were held to mark their centenary. Parts of the system have disappeared, of course – many remember the ceasing of the Marton system in 1962, to be replaced by buses – but the resort's trams continue to be the biggest attraction after the Pleasure Beach and Tower.

## Flights of Fancy

Whereas trams are a form of transport connected firmly to earth, Blackpool enjoys its own airport and, indeed, at one time had two. The history of the airport can be traced to 1909 when the resort proudly staged Britain's first organised air display -pretty impressive when it is realised that this was only six years after the Wright brothers Orville and Wilbur had made their first successful flight near Kitty Hawk in the United States. Aviation seized the public's imagination and Blackpool had to be at the forefront of this newfangled mode of transport. The resort's festival was held at Squires Gate and it is reported that on some days there were crowds of more than 80,000. Among those 'fliers' was one A. V. Roe, whose Avro company went on to become world famous and a household name. In ensuing years no self-respecting seaside resort did not have an Avro plane or two for trips round the area and at Blackpool trips round the Tower were very popular. Alliott Verdon Roe, born in 1877, lived to see aeroplanes become commonplace, for he died in 1958. For another early link with the Blackpool area and aviation, it is interesting to note that John Alcock went to Heyhouses School, St. Annes, leaving when a teenager for Manchester. He was the Alcock who with Arthur Whitten Brown made the historic crossing of the Atlantic in 1919. In later years Amy Johnson and husband Jim Mollison were no strangers to Squires Gate and indeed it was when flying from Squires Gate over the English Channel as a member of the Air Transport Auxiliary that her plane disappeared in 1941.

After the Second World War the future of Squires Gate as an airport did not look very bright. It had been run by the Ministry of Transport and Civil Aviation and within a few years of the

**A Flying Flirtation at Blackpool.**

end of the war it seemed that Squires Gate would close unless Blackpool Corporation were prepared to take it over. The *Blackpool Gazette and Herald* summed up the position neatly in January, 1959, when it posed the questions: 'Can Blackpool afford a three-penny or four-penny rate for an airport which brings few people into the resort? Can Blackpool as a town that ought to have its eye on the future, afford to close the airport?' In the early 1960s the Corporation bought Squires Gate from the Ministry for about £185,000. They appealed for funds from

*Pleasure flights gripped the public imagination in the early years of this century.*

*Pleasure seekers getting a view from above the town.*

FLYING AT BLACKPOOL.

surrounding local authorities, but with little luck. For example, Morecambe Council, which before the war had had visions of having its own airport, refused to donate even a paltry £100.

Through the 1960s and 1970s Blackpool's airport struggled through but, in the face of the ever-burgeoning Manchester Airport – now Manchester International Airport – made little headway. As the 1980s opened, the Council adopted a more aggressive policy, accompanied with the opening of a modern-ised and expanded airport terminal and new business followed. More equipment was brought in to allow aircraft to make more precise runway approaches than with the old radar, meaning fewer days of closure through fog. As the 1980s approached their close, the news for the airport was again uncertain. On April l, 1987, came privatisation along with a concerted 'Fly Blackpool' campaign. The airport had always been somewhat let down by the state of its main runway, so when that was resurfaced in 1988 it was only appropriate that the importance of the occasion should be realised and the official opening ceremony was carried out by Lord Brabazon of Tara, grandson of one of the giants of aviation history. There was an almost immediate upturn in business and as the 1990s dawned new services included regular flights to Palma, Majorca. 'Fly Blackpool' became an option taken by more and more people and there is reason to believe that in the year 2009 the centenary of flying at Blackpool will be a great occasion. Many towns before the second World War had visions of having their own airports. Nearly all have fallen by the wayside. Blackpool has succeeded, demonstrating the courage of the resort's convictions.

## Railway Mania

Finally, as mentioned elsewhere, the railways virtually made Blackpool. But today's presence by comparison is minuscule. The railways came to the

*It's 9.45 a.m outside the old Talbot Road station.*

resort in 1846 and for the next century and a quarter brought millions on holiday and business. A huge railway complex evolved with three stations – Central, North and South. Millions of trippers came on cheap excursion tickets to see the Lights and savour the delights of the sands, Pleasure Beach and Tower. Unfortunately, it did not last. The Second World War took its toll through restrictions on private travelling – 'Is your journey really necessary?' – the post-war 'affluent society' engendered more roads and traffic, and Dr. Beeching with his railway 'axe' got to work in the 1960s. The immense Blackpool Central with its 14 platforms and spaghetti-like network of lines and sidings finally closed on November 2, 1964, though much of the area was left empty and neglected for over 20 years, eventually being made into car and coach parks and amusement complexes. The main line track bed became the base of the M55. With the benefit of hindsight, it is easy to agree with the view expressed by Paul Shannon and John Hillmer in their book 'North West British Railways Past and Present' that: 'It is difficult to believe that such an extensive railway location could be so completely obliterated – and the logic of closing the railway in order to facilitate increased road traffic is highly dubious, to say the least.'

Central Station, opened in 1863 as Hounds Hill and taking the name Central in 1878, was one of the wonders of Blackpool and the Corporation spent nearly a million pounds buying the site following closure. But what has followed hardly has the romance of those days when thousands upon thousands of pasty-faced mill-workers came in from Yorkshire and East Lancashire for their holidays in breezy Blackpool. Most of the railway property became an unsightly mess until redevelopment. The buildings of Blackpool South lingered on until the early months of 1985 when the unofficial efforts of vandals and the official efforts of council workmen finally flattened them. The once fine station had become an unmanned terminus at the end of a single track to Kirkham.

## Fuming in the Traffic

Much of the traffic that was formerly carried by the railways transferred to the roads and the traffic situation in the Blackpool of the 1970s became almost intolerable.

Part of the answer was Yeadon Way from the M55 at Peel Corner through South Shore to Waterloo Road. It was opened in 1986 after a decade of planning and construction work. Costing nearly £5 million, it is named after Harry Yeadon, a former County Council Surveyor who was largely responsible for planning it. Construction of Yeadon Way started on October 1, 1984, when Labour Party Deputy Leader Roy Hattersley cut the first sod, and the first cars were allowed on to the new road on January 3, 1986. The basic route is that of the old Marton railway loop line. The official opening ceremony was carried out by County Councillor George Slynn, Chairman of the County Highways and Transportation Committee.

# 4

## Larger than Life

What an astonishing cavalcade of personalities and 'characters' has Blackpool produced or attracted down the years! The town is an extraordinary, vibrant place and that is well-represented in the folk who have risen to public attention within it. They're not all civic figures or leaders in the entertainment or theatre worlds, too, for every facet of town life has produced outstanding figures, from landau driver to millionaire. In life Blackpool fetes its personalities and, as we shall see, it does so in death, too. Many choose to make their final journey along the Promenade of their beloved town. Such was the case when JACK ALTY died in 1986, for he was carried in his coffin in a glass hearse along the Prom. Jack, who was the best-known landau driver in the resort until he gave up driving his own vehicle a few years before his death, died when aged only 55. He had lived Blackpool heart and soul and not the least of his contributions was in having been founder of the Blackpool Landau Association

in 1980, being its chairman. This organisation has not only done great work in enabling the landau drivers to represent themselves but also for various charities over the years.

This chapter will not be a list of the famous or infamous, the rich and privileged, the do-gooders or good-for-nothings. Another writer no doubt will, one day, produce a comprehensive directory. Here there is room merely to skim the surface and take an almost random glimpse at the multitude. Of hoteliers there have, naturally been scores. One of note was a former Manchester police officer who became one of the resort's best-known hoteliers. HARRY ASHTON came to Blackpool in 1944 to take the appropriately-named Linga Longer guest house in Hornby Road. That was a success and four years later came the purchase of the Atlantic Hotel on North Promenade. Harry threw himself into the life of the hotel and catering side of the town becoming a respected and influential president and Press Officer of the Private Hotels Association, and chairman and Press officer of the Hotel and Catering Liaison Committee. Both these offices put him into the limelight with the media local and national and it could never be said that Harry overlooked an opportunity to promote-and defend the resort. He is remembered not only for his doughty hotels work but for being deeply interested in education and local government, for being a competitive motorist of some skill,including taking part in the RAC Rally, and for organising the first Blackpool Coach Rally. Harry Ashton died in early 1983 having given 40 years' service to the town he loved.

## 'Mr Blackpool'

Well-deserving of the title 'Mr Blackpool' BOB BATTERSBY was for 15 years a Director of Publicity of rare quality. He had a genius for dreaming up stunts and making comments of a headline-making nature, keeping Blackpool constantly in the media spotlight. Bob Battersby could be so good at his job because of an encyclopaedic knowledge of the business, including first-hand experience in the Second World War of acting with such personalities as Arthur Askey and Jack Warner and many others who went on to become household names and performers at Blackpool venues. Bob Battersby made a name for himself in Blackburn in the 1950s putting on concerts at venues such as King Georges Hall, where he negotiated the appearance of such as Ann Shelton, Jimmy Young and Frankie Vaughan, and then moved to lead the publicity department at a town that still likes to consider itself (increasingly unsuccessfully) as a rival to Blackpool – Morecambe. Here, one of the areas he rapidly made his own and an outstanding success was the organisation of the Miss Great Britain contest,then a powerful magnet for holidaymakers. Come the mid-1960s Bob Battersby left the North to go South to Worthing but he returned to Blackpool in 1970 and brilliantly steered the publicity of Britain's leading resort. He retired in 1985, having led one of the most imaginative and innovative publicity and tourism teams the town has seen. He served Blackpool well. It is to be hoped that one day he will write a substantial volume of memoirs, for his job led him to dealing with top politicians, show-business personalities and journalists.

## Clowning around

The name DAVID MAXWELL KING is impressive enough but few will recognise this character until they hear the name that he took in later life – WINDY BLOW. He was the champion of the balloon-twisters, making the balloons into animals and grotesque shapes and even a rather naughty go-go dancer. One of his claims to fame was that he introduced the not usually hilarious

PRINCE CHARLES to the art. When Windy Blow died one of his last wishes was respected and the area was treated to the extraordinary sight of dozens of balloons wafting over Lytham Park Crematorium. Even the funeral car was bedecked with colourful balloons – Blackpool putting on the style. Windy, who at one time had been the head clown in Billy Smart's Circus, got his big break through the Bruce Forsythe show 'The Generation Game.' It is almost bizarre to learn that the way in which this life of blowing balloons started was that Windy had a lung injured in the Second World War and started to blow balloons up to strengthen his lungs. He died, aged 75, in 1988.

Most readers will have heard of the clown the late CHARLIE CAIROLI but probably few know much about the commercial genius of a man who brought Cairoli to the resort. He was CLEMENT BUTSON entertainments manager at the Tower. Butson brought hundreds of acts to that venue but none became so strongly identified with Blackpool, or stayed so long, as Charlie Cairoli. Clement But son, who had already made a name for himself in the late 1920s as publicity and advertising manager for the Tower Company, brought Cairoli to Blackpool in 1939 with his father and brother – and

Charlie stayed for 40 years. A man of remarkable energy and vision, Clement Butson pioneered the Tower Circus with a succession of death-defying acts such as trapeze and high-wire and his work in the 1930s and 1940s pulled in the crowds in their thousands. Until 1947, when he moved to London and entered the world of West End musicals, Clement Butson brought only the best and most imaginative to Blackpool. It is, perhaps, ironic that many remember names of artistes who appeared but few the man who brought them here, often after international negotiations.

Now for CHARLIE CAIROLI himself the very essence of a clown, with red bulbous nose and distinctive bowler hat. He retired officially from the ring in December, 1979 and death came the following February, but the Cairoli tradition continues for his son carries on the clowning. Cairoli, who gave a different presentation every year, appeared before humble folk and royalty, but it made no difference to him. They all got the same performance. The 'clown prince' was aged 70 when he died and of those 70 years he had been a clown for 63, being Italian-born into the circus life. In the brittle and sinister Nazi Germany he even performed before Hitler, who presented him with an inscribed silver cigarette case. It says much for Cairoli that on the day the Second World War broke out he threw the case off North Pier into the sea. Cairoli was a peace-loving man whose personal mission in life was to make the world laugh. He succeeded. He was supported in all he did by his wife for 45 years, Violet, herself an ex-acrobat.

## Wizard of the Wurlitzer

As stated, Bob Battersby earned the title 'Mr. Blackpool' but the man who held that title the longest was without doubt REGINALD DIXON he of the mighty Wurlitzer organ in the Tower Ballroom. For 40 years he reigned supreme over that instrument, the Wizard of the Wurlitzer until the 1970s, but despite being 'Mr. Blackpool' and the Wurlitzer being the epitome of the resort in which millions really do 'like to be beside the seaside,' Reg was not born a local man but in Sheffield. Eventually he ended up in Preston and that town's loss was Blackpool's gain, for Reginald, who married his wife Vera in Preston, was sacked from the New Victoria there (what a short-sighted decision that was!) and moved to Blackpool in 1930. It was 1970 before he left the Wurlitzer for the last time, a lifetime devoted to music and the resort, whose name makes one think still of that Wurlitzer rising majes-

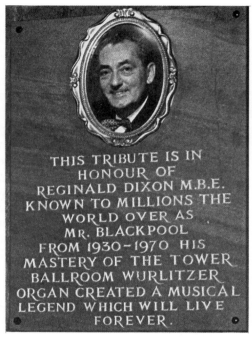

*A slate plaque erected at the Tower to the memory of Reginald Dixon, the man who for so many years ruled over the mighty Wurlitzer organ and who made 'I do like to be beside the seaside' the anthem of the resort. He designed the Wurlitzer himself and was its master for 40 years.*

THIS TRIBUTE IS IN HONOUR OF REGINALD DIXON M.B.E. KNOWN TO MILLIONS THE WORLD OVER AS MR. BLACKPOOL FROM 1930-1970 HIS MASTERY OF THE TOWER BALLROOM WURLITZER ORGAN CREATED A MUSICAL LEGEND WHICH WILL LIVE FOREVER.

tically for an extravaganza of musical fun. The music lingers on and so does the memory and appreciation of Reginald Dixon's vast contribution to the history of Blackpool. Perhaps it is a little odd that his seaside organist's career should have come from a family of strict Methodist principles. Reginald Dixon, who lived in Poulton-le-Fylde, a little way out of Blackpool, and who had the Wurlitzer built to his own design, died in May, 1985.

He was made an MBE in 1966 and the

Queen is known to have been one of his fans. Tributes flooded in from throughout Britain and overseas. As a matter of fact, when in 1970 Reginald Dixon retired from the Tower, he did not desert the organ as an instrument though he deliberately did not return to play at the Tower. He gave concerts around the country, buoyed up by the increasing popularity of home organs. Blackpool's anthem is 'I do like to be beside the seaside' and Reginald was the man who made it so. He died, much mourned, at the age of 80.

The characters come down through the years. Some are the effervescent personalities of show-business, others more sober figures, the ones who handled the finance and planning that put more colourful people into the public view. WILLAIM HENRY HAIGH SMITH was such a one, a largely behind-the-scenes character but one who, in his field of expertise, had an important influence on Blackpool. His story is not quite one of rags to riches but it is certainly of that genre and is a commercial romance of the Tower and Winter Gardens. William Henry Haigh Smith rose from being a programme seller when a schoolboy to being an important company secretary. Until the late 1930s the Tower Company and Winter Gardens Company were separate entities. Smith as a lad sold programmes at the Tower, joined the company full-time when he left school aged about 13 rose through the ranks to become secretary and became so highly thought of that when the Tower and Winter Gardens companies merged, he kept the position. Many years later came the takeover by EMI and he continued with the new company. He died, aged 86, in 1979. A kindly man who never married, he had retired in the late 1950s. By his will he left substantial sums to various charities including the Salvation Army, Help the Aged, Oxfam and Barnardos.

## Big names in Blackpool

Some names live on in the public mind, others, for one reason or another, fade. One that should occupy a more prominent position is, LAWRENCE WRIGHT a man of great talent who for over 30 years presented a hugely popular show at the North Pier – 'On With the Show.' He started the show in the halcyon days between the First and Second World Wars, the days of blazers and straw boaters and when it never seemed to rain during long, hot English summers. These were the days of Jazz and the Charleston, of 'Bright Young Things' with short skirts and bobbed hair. Lawrence Wright started his North

Pier show in 1924 and the records show that almost anybody who was anybody in show-business knew Wright and appeared in the shows. He was a prolific song-writer and publicist. His most memorable stunt was perhaps when he was pushing the song 'I've Never Seen a Straight Banana' and declared he would give £1,000 to anyone who could produce one! Some of his titles are still immediately recognised – 'Among My Souvenirs,' 'Gipsy Melody' and 'Shepherds of the Hills' among them. It did not hurt, of course, that he was the founder of *The Melody Maker* magazine and was in a perfect position to promote his own material, which he often did under various names he used as a composer. It was 'on with the show' for Wright from 1924 until his retirement in 1956. The Leicester-born genius died in Blackpool in 1964. He adopted Blackpool and Blackpool most certainly took him to its heart. The flag on the North Pier was flown at half-mast during his funeral.

The memory of a large sum being offered in connection with a bizarre 'find' is also associated with a character of slightly later times. The hallmark of the showmen of Blackpool is always to recognise the main chance. Such a man was BERNARD WOOLLEY, who died in 1985. In the late 1960s he offered £10,000 to anyone who discovered the Loch Ness Monster, his intention being to exhibit 'Nessie' on the Golden Mile. The money was never paid, of course, but Woolley's challenge was a reminder that the resort has never lost the link with the early days of side shows and freak exhibits and that a yen for this kind of entertainment lurks beneath what is but a thin veneer of sophistication. One of his extremely successful exhibits was 'The Man With the X-Ray Eyes', a recurring and highly profitable theme. This sort of thing really would have been better placed in the earlier, rougher, tougher days of the original Golden Mile, the days of THE RECTOR OF STIFFKEY (see later) and one suspects that if Woolley had operated 25 or 30 years earlier he would have become even more successful.

Among those who have helped cater for the entertainment needs not only of the resort but the country as a whole, the name PETER WEBSTER is in the top league. He gave dozens of up and coming stars their first big break in his Summer shows at the Central and South Piers and when he retired in 1982 could look back with pride not only on having produced top-line shows but having set on the road to stardom the likes of Ken Dodd, The Bachelors and Morecambe and Wise. As with so many other leading personalities in Blackpool, he was a 'foreigner' to the town, a Londoner who first made his mark here by producing children's shows that are an affectionate memory for thousands who recall 'Uncle Peter.' But a far cry from those children's shows was that Peter Webster was also producer of 'Randle's Summer Scandals' in 1952, a show that lived up fully to its title. Webster, who in 1982 after retirement headed for the sunshine of Tenerife, had few regrets after a lifetime in show-business – but there was one at least. He had had the chance to sign up the Beatles just before they became famous but had not realised their potential. He spent about 40 years at the Central and South Piers and in that time came into contact with a galaxy of stars – Mike Yarwood, The Grumbleweeds, Camberwick Green, Roy Castle, Jimmy James, Josef Locke, Jimmy Clitheroe, Al Read, indeed almost a 'Who's Who' of those who were to become household names in years to follow. They all had much to thank 'Uncle Peter' for. It is not surprising that Peter Webster displayed such brilliance, for he was born into the business, in Battersea where his father earned a living as a whistler in the music halls. Peter Webster came to Blackpool after demob from the RAF.

The names of the great and the rather more humble jostle for attention in the annals of the town. For years show-business funerals were held at the 'actors' church' St. Stephen's-on-the-Cliffs. There are many memorials there, some to the very famous. In 1930, for instance, the widows of the famous dancing master JOHN TILLER and JOHN HUDDLESTONE, an outstanding general manager of the Winter Gardens, gave a stained glass window in memory of their husbands. It was unveiled in the Actors' Chapel by another great personality, SIR JOHN BICKERSTAFFE, chairman of the Tower Company. As we say, the more humble jostle for attention with the better known. DORIS TAYLOR should be mentioned. Doris Taylor?

Well, she deserves mention because she, perhaps unwittingly, became a 'women's lib' pioneer in the resort. In the dark days of the Second World War, in August, 1940, she joined the Corporation's Transport Department as a trainee and in 1942 became the town's first woman bus driver. She died, aged 67, in 1982.

Local politics have produced many great figures but there is no intention in 'Reflections' to plod through a list of local worthies. That has been done before many times. Go to the local libraries and their shelves groan under the weight of mighty and detailed tomes

– often largely unread – of the great and good. Instead, we shall pick out two, the first Labour Mayor and the first woman Mayor.

The first Labour Mayor was ERNEST MACHIN who died, aged 93, in 1983. He became a prominent 'Labourite' in the stormy days of the 1930s, days of slump and unemployment when the signs of the approaching Second World War were making themselves apparent. He came to hold many posts, including Leader of Blackpool Labour Party and President of the local Trades Council, a magistrate and a CBE. He was Mayor of Blackpool 1959-60 and received overdue recognition when he was made a Freeman of Blackpool in 1973. Despite all this success, he was a man of only partially fulfilled ambition for he twice unsuccessfully stood as Parliamentary candidate for the constituency. Had he got into Parliament, Ernie Machin would undoubtedly have gone on to have had a high profile political career and very probably ended up in the Lords. Indeed, many believe he was the 'best Lord Blackpool never had.' But he stayed on the local scene and carved out an equally impressive local career, remaining always plain 'Ernie' to his friends. The first woman Mayor, who achieved also the historical footnote of having been the resort's first woman alderman,

was JEAN ROBINSON, who died in 1987 at the age of 87. She was Mayor 1968-9 in the days prior to local government reorganisation. As with Ernie Machin, she was a lifelong supporter of the Labour Party, with her husband Noel. Her death saw the close of a period of public service from 1933, when she and Noel came to the resort to open a cafe in the Abingdon Market which they ran until the late 1960s.

Many people in Blackpool down the years have ascribed at least part of their success to the education they received at one of the town's leading schools, Arnold. The school, dating to 1896, was founded by a man of exceptional vision and astuteness, FRANK TRUSWELL PENNINGTON, and Arnold school has always maintained its reputation for quality and innovation. Considering his influence on the town the surprise is, perhaps, that Pennington was not a Blackpool-born man but sprang from near Newark on Trent in 1872, coming here in the 1890s, a period of extraordinary and heady growth in Blackpool's history, one in which were laid the foundations of much that we see even today. Pennington adopted the town and though a struggling teacher with little money, was recognised by many parents as a man of special ability and presence and within only a few years he was successful enough to found his own school. This occupied premises in one or two locations before he took over what had been the buildings of Arnold House School. The venture met with success from the start and Pennington also involved himself in many aspects of Blackpool's public life. The local story is that he arrived in town with worldly goods to the value of only about £5 and from that humble start grew to virtually call the shots in the resort's educational development and became a wealthy and influential figure. He died in 1938, four years after his wife and devoted helpmate Annie, and is remembered for his business acumen, for being a strict disciplinarian who knew what he wanted and usually got it, and for his single-mindedness of purpose. He strides through the pages of the education history of the town. With generous moustache and firm Methodist ideals, he even looked like a pioneer. Why Arnold School? The name comes from Thomas Arnold, the famous head of Rugby School.

These early years in the resort saw the springing forth of many notable public figures and one who must be mentioned is SIR LINDSEY PARKINSON who rose to be head of a great civil engineering company but who is remembered as much for having been president and chairman of Blackpool Football Club. Parkinson, who died in February, 1936, aged 65 at Blackpool, was three times Mayor of the resort, honorary Freeman, chairman and president of the cricket club as well as the football club, and town pioneer. Starting in a small way with his father as a builder and contractor, the business grew and during the First World War the firm carried out Army contracts running into millions of pounds and later its civil engineering activities became world-wide. In 1935, when Morecambe was to build its Olympic-sized Super Swimming Stadium, the town, arch-rival of Blackpool, awarded the contract to Sir Lindsay Parkinson's firm because, simply, it was the best-equipped for the job. The firm carried out great contracts throughout the world. British contracts that are memorable include the £2.5 million Liverpool – Manchester road opened in 1934 by the King, and Grimsby Docks. Abroad the contracts included building a new dock and harbour at Oporto, Portugal, costing £1m, a new harbour at Jersey and dock schemes in Cyprus. During one of his terms as Mayor of Blackpool, Parkinson dropped a bombshell when he bought the Blackpool – Fleetwood tram route before anyone else realised it was for sale and promptly offered it at the same price to the Corporation, commenting:

'If you don't want it, I'll run it myself.' The Council accepted his offer with alacrity. He was a man of huge talent who, despite becoming rich and famous, retained the knack of mixing happily with ordinary folk. He was a revered figure at the football and cricket clubs and had been no mean sportsman himself in his younger days, having played for the old South Shore side before its amalgamation with Blackpool in 1899. Robin Daniels, in his excellent 'Blackpool Football: The official club history', reports an interview with Peter Doherty that sums up Parkinson's attitude to the club.

> 'Sir Lindsay Parkinson, Blackpool's Chairman, had practically taken over the club. He was a wonderful person. Once, when he was ill, he sent for me. He said, "Peter, remember these words. While I'm alive you will not leave this club." And I said, "I never want to leave Blackpool, sir." He once said to me, "I will look after you when your playing days are over. You can work in my firm." I was very happy at Blackpool.'

Of course, the club in later years was home to many of modern sporting history's legendary names, but few are so revered as the late STAN MORTEN-SEN – 'Morty' to his many fans. The opening years of the 1990s robbed us of that great character. His 1953 FA Cup Medal was one of his most treasured possessions, and rightly so, for it was he who scored the only hat-trick recorded in a Wembley Final. It was a thrilling game. Blackpool, in the First Division, were in their third Cup Final and were behind 3 – 1 to Bolton. There were 20 minutes still to play and 'Morty,' playing alongside other geniuses like Stanley Matthews, came up trumps.

The first decades of the present century were of frantic development of Blackpool and it took civic leaders of rare quality and vision to propel and sustain that progress. In 1910 the Liberal W H BROADHEAD became Mayor for the second-time. He was Mayor first in 1905-6, having been elected to the Council in 1896. He was head of Broadhead Theatres, which were scattered over the busy cities and towns of Lancashire, and also, along with his son, was owner of the Winter Gardens. W. H. became Mayor for the second time at an auspicious time in the resort's history, for there were to be the Coronation festivities, the opening of the new Carnegie Library and the completion of important Promenade works.

An outstanding Mayor a few years later was TOM BICKERSTAFFE. He was Mayor in 1926 when Blackpool became a

Borough, he having first joined the Council in 1891. The words of a certificate issued to the new borough's school pupils sum up the spirit of this great pioneer. 'The growth of the Borough has been due to the ideals and deeds of many men and women of good will who, moved by civic patriotism, have devoted their energies and ability to advance the progress of the town they loved. Blackpool as it exists today forms an enduring monument to the genius and self-sacrifice of those pioneers and builders and their memory should be a source of inspiration and pride to those who follow them.' When he died in 1934 it is recorded that nearly 50,000 lined the Promenade to pay their respects as his ashes were scattered at sea.

Does the name Brendan Rosbotham mean anything to you? Probably not. Nor will it to many Blackpool people. But when it is realised that it was the real name of entertainer BRIAN ROSSI, recognition is immediate. Rossi was an entertainer who, with his bald head and Fu Manchu moustache, cut a striking figure on the entertainment scene and over the years appeared at most of the venues in the resort and other towns like Morecambe, Fleetwood and Cleveleys. A heart attack snatched Brian Rossi from life at the young age of 49. Ironically the Irishman – he was born in Belfast and came to Blackpool in the 1960s – was on the brink of entering the international 'big time' for he was due to go to the United States for cabaret contracts in Los Angeles and New York.

The resort put on the style for Rossi's funeral in 1984. He lay in 'state' in a white coffin in his stage suit and was driven in a white Rolls-Royce to the Sacred Heart Roman Catholic Church. He was taken from life at a young age and almost a year later to the day another personality fell victim to heart attack at an even younger age. He was BARRY NOBLE , who operated a chain of amusement centres across the North and Midlands and who built up an almost cult following with his radio adverts in which his 'Geordie' accent boomed out. Noble loved to project the image of the 'rough diamond' but in fact he was a very astute businessman indeed. At one time he owned three major centres on the Central Promenade in Blackpool alone. In some towns, one of the ways in which he placated planning authorities who were concerned about the possible garishness of his premises, was to decorate the windows with rather elegant classical sculptures. He became a great figure on the Golden Mile, living life to the full. He died in the Isle of Man.

Having mentioned one 'rough diamond,' it is appropriate here perhaps to mention another, JACK PYE, who boasted being the oldest wrestler in the country. Jack wrestled until he was 60 and on his retirement in 1964 looked back on a career involving over 5,000 contests, many of them televised. He appeared at scores of leading venues in addition to Blackpool – Belle Vue at Manchester and Wigan's Springfield Road among them – and for all his ring persona, Jack had a heart of gold. Every year in Blackpool he played the part of Father Christmas to local orphans at parties. He wrestled his way to the very top of the sport in the years when wrestling was almost a religion for its fans. Twenty-five thousand watched him fight Billy Riley for the World Championship, a world record audience, and he wrestled in many foreign countries, appeared in films alongside such stars as Diana Dors, and had a long-remembered club in Blackpool. He was a big man with a big heart.

Occupying a place in the affections of all Blackpudlians was VIOLET CARSON, remembered always as the 'Ena Sharples' of 'Coronation Street' but who had other careers before she became embedded in the public's consciousness as the 'Dragon of The Street.' Manchester-born Violet, daughter of a flour-mill manager, displayed show-business pro-

mise from the start and it was her good fortune to pick up a job as a silent-cinema pianist, which gave her a good grounding for a musical career that was to follow. Her first radio broadcast came in the 1920s when she broadcast with her sister Nellie and she went on to become a household name in radio shows such as 'Have a Go,' with the inimitable Wilfred Pickles, 'Variety Bandbox' and 'Woman's Hour.' But she was known most affectionately to legions of children as 'Auntie Vi' in 'Children's Hour.'

Living in Bispham, Violet enjoyed a career in drama in the years that followed, appearing in some of the leading roles of playwrights such as J.B. Priestley and Willis Hall, and she successfully crossed over to television, where she excelled. Her dramatic roles included Shakespeare (Duchess of York, in *Richard the Third*) and in 1961 she was voted Britain's Best Character Actress on television. It was in that year that Granada, in an inspired choice of casting, offered her the role of Ena Sharples in the then formative Coronation Street. The rest, as they say, is history.

Violet, who played a high-profile role in the public events of Blackpool, travelled to Manchester several times a week to mould the part into one of the best-loved on British television, and she

*A lovely picture of the Church Street entrance of the Winter Gardens complex from a postcard postmarked October 7, 1907. There is a line of landaus left of centre and on the right the mighty, but short-lived, Gigantic Wheel towers above the chimney pots. On the back of the card is a prosaic message from one M. Margerison to Mrs. Cowell, Eaves Green, Goosnargh, Preston: 'Will you bring or send the damsons I bought to Alston Hall on Wednesday.'*

was for many years the rock upon which the programme stood. To many, from 1961 to near the end of her life, she WAS Ena Sharples, but in fact her real character was the very opposite. She died on Boxing Day, 1983, aged 85, following a long illness, and when her funeral service was conducted in a packed Bispham Parish Church, the Rector, the Rev. David Maddock, spoke for all when he said: 'Here in Bispham and Blackpool, we think of her with affection as someone who never forgot her local community. She always had time for those causes that would help and encourage others.' Violet had been a regular worshipper at the church and at one period was a member of the choir. At a memorial service at Manchester Cathedral, William Roache (Coronation Street's Ken Barlow) commented: 'Violet belonged to that unique group of special people to whom God had granted the ability to bring pleasure to each and every one of the seven ages of man... From the very young to the very old, we have all been touched by her magic. We loved her as Auntie Vi or Ena or that wonderful pianist of Have a Go or the dramatic actress of The Age of Kings or the talented accompanist and singer that she undoubtedly was.' In July, 1989, the bungalow where Violet Carson lived until her death was sold at auction for £85,700. It is opposite playing fields in Fleetwood Road, Bispham. Of course Blackpool has received many mentions in the scripts of Coronation Street – for where else would one go on a trip from the grimy industrial towns and cities of the North? Sometimes the resort has been used as an integral part of the programme' plot. This was the case in 1989, for instance, when Coronation Street villain Allan Bradley (played by Mark Eden) met his end after being knocked down by a Bispham-bound tram. Fans of the programme will remember that he went to Blackpool in search of his former lover, Rita Fairclough.

In 1985, on premises belonging to the Ismail tea and coffee merchants in Cocker Street, North Shore, the chairman and chief executive of Jaguar Cars unveiled a plaque to the memory of SIR WILLIAM LYONS. By no stretch of the imagination is Blackpool at the hub of the mighty automobile industry, and few outside the immediate area realise

that the origins of that most famous of marques, Jaguar, are to be found in the resort. When John Egan unveiled that plaque it was a reminder that the rather mundane premises were the headquarters of the Swallow Side Car Company, which from the early 1920s had switched from place to place in Blackpool – Bloomfield Road, just across the railway from the football ground, and on the corner of John Street and Moon Avenue -until taking up residence for two years at Cocker Street in 1926. Later the company moved to Coventry to become the Jaguar of fame. To motoring enthusiasts, the names of the early products are still revered, among them the Austin Swallow, which was a two-seater Austin Swallow body on the chassis of the Austin Seven. The full name of the firm was the Swallow Side Car and Coach Building Company and when the move to Coventry took place in 1928 about 50 were working for it and many are known to have moved to Coventry, thus extending Blackpool's roots to the Midlands. William Lyons was born in Blackpool in 1901 and attended Poulton-le-Fylde Grammar School and Arnold School. After making Jaguar into one of the leading marques, he died in Rugby in 1985, aged 84. His character was summed up well in the book 'The Motor Makers,' by Martin Adeney, published three years after his death. 'William Lyons was to be one of the most complete of the great figures of the British motor industry – a brilliant conceptual designer who would whittle away at a piece of wood to provide the shape he wanted, but was always involved with every detail of his factory organisation from the intricacies of the wage rates to the exact positioning of instruments on a dashboard. Years after his death, the company's cars still bore his recognisable imprint... In spite of the flamboyance of has cars, Lyons remained studiously unassuming, in keeping with the frugality he valued. He was formal, if not cold, addressing long-serving workers as Mr. or Mrs., but he was as single-minded and tough with employers and Governments as he could be with workers. There was no design team to speak of; it remained Lyons, and even small decisions on his cars could not be taken if he was away. That was as much the case at the end as it was at the modest start.'

The Golden Mile – which was never more than a gilt half-mile – had its golden age in the 1920s and 1930s, and today's Golden Mile, mostly rebuilt only a few years ago, bears little resemblance to the rip-roaring days of freak shows and animal acts. All who know anything about Blackpool's past will have heard

of the notorious Rector of Stiffkey; more of him later; but fewer will recall one of his predecessors from an era when the Golden Mile had a succession of fasting men and women. Some of the so-called fasting was mere cheating but other times it was real and on one occasion at least led to death. This was the case with THE GREAT SACCO, or Saccho, whose real name was Richard Hans Jone. Riccardo Sacco was a protege of LUKE GANNON, one of the pioneers of the Golden Mile, a brilliant entrepreneur who exploited the pull of mawkish interest. In 1929 Gannon set up The Great Sacco in a glass case, and there he resided for no fewer than 65 days, ogled at by a public who bet with each other on how long he could last out. Sacco became extremely ill and died soon after the feat. He left estate valued at probate at just £44 4s. 10d. Luke Cannon was an East Lancashire man, having been born in Burnley. A character of well-developed vocal abilities, he became a Sergeant Major in the First World War. After the war he abandoned his trade of cotton weaver and came to the Central Beach and the Golden Mile, where his shows attracted thousands of people a day. Gannon died in 1939, one of the great pioneering spirits of the Golden Mile.

For a town that makes news constantly, it is no surprise that many leading journalists have been born here or adopted Blackpool for their careers. ARTHUR FIRTH, for instance, became Editor of the *Daily Express*. The education he received at Blackpool Grammar School and Arnold School no doubt stood him in good stead for the rough and tumble of national journalism. He died in December, 1987, a lifetime in newspapers behind him. A local character was BRIAN COLLINS, who for nearly a quarter of a century was Sports Editor of the *West Lancs Evening Gazette*, Blackpool's own widely-respected evening newspaper. He cut his teeth on weekly newspapers in the area before joining the Gazette. He was a great loss to the sporting scene when he died in May, 1988. But perhaps the newspaperman who most will remember from recent years was SIR HAROLD GRIME, for he was Editor of the West Lancs Evening Gazette from the time it was launched in 1929 – and he was still contributing to the paper on his death at the age of 88 in August, 1984. Knighted in 1959 he had a distinguished career both inside and outside newspapers, was an author, director of the Tower and Winter Gardens Company, Deputy Lieutenant of the County, chairman of the Press Association and director of Reuters among many, many other posts and interests. A great newspaperman

and an astute businessman – the two rarely coincide! As with so many, part of his education was at Arnold School.

There is little intention in 'Reflections' to hearken back much to pre-20th century days but there is one pioneer who must not be omitted from any work on Blackpool, so extraordinary was his life. The REV WILLIAM THORNBER, who died in 1885, wrote a bulky and fascinating history of Blackpool in its formative years. A brilliant historian, he was not so successful in general life. His marriage fell apart, he took to drink, was dismissed from the Church for drunkenness, resorted to fisticuffs to settle arguments with parishioners and ended his days in a Staffordshire mental institution, aged 82. Despite his stormy life, his 1837-published history of Blackpool is arguably the best written on the early years of the resort and fortunately a reprint was published on the centenary of his death.

It seems that Ministers of uncertain pedigree have something of a penchant for the resort, for it was an expelled rector who some half-century later became a leading attraction on the Golden Mile. HAROLD FRANCIS DAVIDSON, alias the RECTOR OF STIFFKEY, in Norfolk, got into trouble with the Church authorities over his alleged activities to 'save' ladies of the night in

London's West End. His liking for the ladies resulted in a scandalous story emerging at a Consistory Court and in 1932 he was unfrocked in Norwich Cathedral. Davidson adopted another pulpit, a barrel on the Golden Mile in which he claimed he would starve himself until his innocence was proved. Thousands flocked to see him, the draw of an unfrocked clergyman who had been associated with prostitutes being irresistible to the thrill-seeking crowds. But the sensation did not last long. Within a year or two those crowds became satiated – there was always another bizarre attraction on the Golden Mile in those days – and the Rector of Stiffkey became merely a figure of ridicule, with his campaign to prove his innocence ignored, his stunts becoming more and more outrageous. He left Blackpool and, entirely appropriately, he was mauled by a lion at Skegness in 1937 and died. He was buried at Stiffkey. Davidson really was an extraordinary character. In 1932 his antics led to his mentor, Luke Gannon, described earlier, being fined £2 by the resort's magistrates for causing an obstruction with the barrel. Gannon didn't mind. Hundreds of holidaymakers thronged round the attraction. They paid 2d. for admission and up to £100 a day was taken at the door. As a matter of fact,

the authorities had a dismal time in trying to control Gannon and Davidson. On one occasion Davidson was charged by Blackpool police with attempted suicide. Davidson won the case. Later he sued the Corporation and won £382 damages and costs.

People say sometimes the thrill-seeking spectacle has disappeared from the modern resort but surely the antics of Californian KINNIE GIBSON in 1986 at the Tower fall into the same category as the old days. Gibson strapped a jet-pack to his back and was rocketed 100 ft. up the Tower at 60 mph. You just don't find that sort of thing happening in other resorts: Or how about CAL CALINI? Three years earlier he was shackled with chains and padlocks in an underwater tomb, a replica of the one used by the great Harry Houdini, himself no stranger to Blackpool. And what of KARL BARTONI? In the same year he made a succession of escapes while bound 100 ft. in the air and hanging from a burning rope. Just to make it that little bit more exciting, Karl and his partner, LIZ MACDOUGAL, hanging upside down beneath him. The crowd loved it and the old Golden Mile philosophy was shown to be alive and well. Bartoni even had the crowds in suspense for his wedding in 1985, for he and Wendy Stokes were married 400 feet up

Blackpool Tower while on a platform hanging from a cable. As the witty headline in the *West Lancs Evening Gazette* put it, it was 'High Do.' All this was very much in the tradition of perhaps the last of the old-style great escapologists, Norman Carrington Walters – better known as MURRAY – who ended his days at Blackpool in 1988, many saying he had been the equal in skill and fame of Houdini.

Now a return to rather less sensational characters. We have already mentioned one of Blackpool's landau drivers, Jack Alty, and it would be a serious omission to neglect to mention another, JOHNSON MONKMAN,who decided in 1989 that it was time for him to retire. After all, he was 88 and had been driving landaus since the First World War. A Blackpudlian to the hilt, he was taught the art by his father and Johnson, who when he retired was the longest-serving landau driver in Blackpool, himself became one of the attractions of the town. The landaus of Blackpool carry on – there are over 40 of them and no trip to the town is really complete without a ride in one – but it is doubtful if we will see Johnson Monkman's record beaten.

Many will remember JAMES WALTON, who was an 'ice cream king' of the resort, but perhaps fewer will recall his deep and abiding love of the Lake District and the fact that he ended up owning part of one of the most beautiful lakes. Walton, of Queen's Square, started with one shop and went on to build up to a score of shops and cafes. In 1957 he became owner of part of Derwentwater following an auction of some of the holdings of the late Lord Leconfield. Walton bought part of the lake near Brandlehow on the Western shore. His attitude to spending what was then a substantial sum of money summed up the character of the man. He said: 'I came to the sale because I like sales. Then halfway through I thought I'd like to buy the lake. I get tired of the tide at Blackpool. It always goes out. I thought it would be nice to have a tide that always stays still. And as I like water. I was prepared to bid up to £3,000'. (*Lancashire Evening Post*, July 18, 1957). In fact, he paid £500, outbidding by £25 New York fur manufacturer Marco Sinai.

Links with the pioneers of Blackpool continue into modern times. Many probably did not realise that when in June, 1983, a 95-year-old woman died in the resort, she was the last surviving of the eight children of Sir John Bickerstaffe. She was DAISEY VICTORIA BAIRD, and her father, as has already been noticed, rose to become 'father' of the Council, chairman of the Tower Company, Freeman of Blackpool and an influential figure throughout the North West. He was a man who was involved in nearly every facet of Blackpool's rise as a resort – but was equally as famed for his clipped beard, moustache and yachting cap. A jaunty figure indeed!

Of show business their number is legion, of course. GRACIE FIELDS was a true friend of Blackpool. Much of her famous 'Sing As We Go' film was made in the resort. Anybody who was anybody, it seems, has switched on the Illuminations. JANE MANSFIELD did so in 1959. BETTE DAVIS visited here at least twice. Of clowns there have been many. Charlie Cairoli, the greatest, has already been referred to, but many also remember the likes of SPATZ the Tower Circus clown whose real name was plain Eric Moore. JOSEF LOCKE , the big Irish tenor who has recently come into the public domain again as a result of a film of his life story, appeared at Blackpool many times, indeed lived here, before disappearing to Southern Ireland, and the film, 'Hear My Song,' has been a reminder of what a wonderful voice this man has. Locke's financial predicaments became well known and when he fled to Ireland the authorities knew full well where he was, they just couldn't get at him. A warrant for his arrest was issued at the Blackpool Bankruptcy Court in November, 1958, when the Registrar, Mr. W. J. Plant, scathingly commented: 'This bankrupt has absconded and is now in Southern Ireland. He is well aware of the court order to be here this morning.' That warrant was issued in Locke's real name of Joseph McLaughlin.

Many in Blackpool will know the name ANGERLINA PETULENGRO the world-famous clairvoyant. She once helped the writer, then the struggling editor of the tiny *Garstang Courier* weekly newspaper, by providing a horoscope column without any unforeseen costs – and thus earning a lasting place in his affections! Remember WINIFRED ATWELL the Trinidadian pianist whose smile was one of the brightest on stage and screen as she shifted her considerable frame on to the piano stool. She appeared in Blackpool on several occasions from the 1950s to the 1970s and she belted out the boogie-woogie for capacity audiences – a lady of ample proportions and enormous charm who endeared herself to all before her death at the age of 69 in 1983. In the same category of larger-than-life characters was the handlebar-moustached JIMMY 'WHACKO' EDWARDS who despite coming to Blackpool on several occasions, declared that the resort was a 'den of men and whores and drink' and that the Tower was a 'monument to sin.' Was he serious. Jimmy Edwards is now dead and it was rarely easy to tell when he was being serious about anything.

Naturally over the years there have been some pretty rum characters on the stages of the resort. Two major names spring to mind immediately – FRANK RANDEL and GEORGE FORMBY. The latter was the toothy, grinning, ukelele-strumming comedian for whom life did not always 'turn out nice again.' Wigan-born, the son of George Formby senior, who made the original Wigan Pier joke, George junior rose to great wealth, appearing on stages and in films throughout the world. But he was always firmly under the thumb of his wife Beryl, who ruled every minute of his life. George, who died in Preston, captured the affections of the common people with his risque songs and jokes. We all know what he was on about when he sang his 'Cleaning Windows' song, or 'A Little Bit of Blackpool Rock,' but somehow he managed to get the material to pass the local Watch Committees and censors when many other entertainers fell foul of the blue pencil. George projected himself as a gormless Lancashire lad but was nothing of the kind in reality and always wanted to break away from the strictures of his wife. The way in which he finally did

*Angerlina Petulengro, clairvoyant who helped the writer.*

has gone down in local legend. Beryl had cancer of the womb and succumbed to the disease on Christmas Day at St. Annes in 1960. Seven weeks later George proclaimed that he was engaged to a Preston school teacher he had known for many years. Consternation! Scandal! The national and local Press had a field day. However, it was a union destined for disaster. George and Pat Howson set up home at Lea, near Preston, she sporting a prominent diamond engagement ring. But George became ill, the marriage plans fell apart and George died at the young age of 56 in 1961, a giant of show business whose passing was mourned internationally. For a decade Pat How son enjoyed the fame – notoriety – of having been George's intended but she then died of cancer at the age of 46 in 1971. Local people remember much acrimony and sourness after George's death concerning his fortune but it was demonstrated that his heart had been in the right place when it was found that a great deal of his money had been left to various charities. His memory lingers on. Blackpool has a thriving George Formby appreciation society.

The life of FRANK RANDLE was also tinged with tragedy and it was at Blackpool that he died at the Queen's Theatre in 1957. Those who knew, or knew of, Randle and his show 'Randle's Summer Scandals,' will never forget him. He was, quite simply, the most outrageous comedian of his time, his double entendres being legendary. Randle, like Formby, was a product of Wigan but when a boy came to Blackpool, a resort with whose public morality guardians he waged a war of attrition to the end of his days. A professional Northerner, Randle built a whole career out of thinly-disguised, and sometimes not disguised at all, smut – and the public loved it! His behaviour off-stage was as outrageous as on. He consistently ignored official warnings to tone down his scripts, hired an aeroplane and dropped toilet rolls on Blackpool to express his opinion of the authorities, made several court appearances for drunken behaviour, was frequently involved in late-night escapades, lost his driving licence through drink and ended his days suffering, among other illnesses, cirrhosis of the liver. He died riddled with alcohol and painkillers. Randle was paid vast sums and lost the lot several times over. A real rags to riches to rags story, what really ended Randle as a comedian, apart from his drinking, was that his Northern humour did not travel well. South Eastern audiences especially did not take to the professional Northerner, a fate that awaited many as in the late

1950s the number of live theatres started to dwindle and commercial television came in. The BBC always took a dim view of this scallywag, most of the time pointedly ignoring him. Neither Blackpool nor the country as a whole is likely to experience again the likes of Frank Randle.

The South Shore at Blackpool is commonly held to have the biggest concentration of hotels and guest houses in Europe. Not the least responsible for this accolade was a woman whom the Blackpool papers in the 1920s and 1930s dubbed the 'Queen of Hotels.' She was MAUD BOURNE, who started out with a £20 legacy and went on to become one of the greatest hotel builders in both Blackpool and the rival resort of Morecambe. Oldham-born, she used that £20 left in the will of an aunt to open a draper's shop in the South Yorkshire mining village of South Elmsall, later moving to Scarborough to run a boarding-house. From there she moved to Blackpool and entered the world of high finance by buying a strip of land on the South Shore, to build hotels where previously there had been nothing but sand. In all, she built about 100 hotels and boarding-houses in the resort before leaving for Morecambe where she adopted a similar strategy in that resort's East End, including the building of More-cambe's Broadway Hotel, opened in 1937. In later life Maud Bourne bought other hotels in the North West, including Warton Grange, near Carnforth, and the Albion Hotel, Arnside. She died, at the grand old age of 99, at Warton, near Carnforth, just before Christmas 1983.

With the next entry, are we talking about one or two? The ventriloquist TERRY HALL developed a soft spot for Blackpool, for it was in 1950 when he was appearing in one of the pier shows, that he paid a visit to the Tower Zoo and spotted a rather morose-looking lion. It gave him the idea that evolved into LENNY THE LION but it was no overnight success, being originally a flop. A change of the voice on the advice of singer, ANN SHELTON, who was also appearing in Blackpool, produced the desired results.

This chapter should not end without reference to a controversial Chief Constable of Blackpool, STANLEY PARR. Parr was a brilliant policeman who served in various parts of the county from 1937 to 1977. During the Second World War he was commissioned in the R.N.V.R. and was in the assault landing craft forces during the initial landings in Normandy, later seeing active service in the Far East on mine-sweeper operations. In 1962, at the age of 45, he became Chief Constable of Blackpool, going on to become Chief Constable of Lancashire in 1971. Unfortunately, despite a distinguished career, he became involved in controversy and was found guilty in December, 1977, of malpractice, largely as the result of a concerted Press campaign. Many who knew Parr considered he had been harshly treated. In his younger days he was a fine sportsman, a Rugby football enthusiast and he was founder of the Lancashire Constabulary Rugby team. He died in 1985.

# 5

# Facts and Fallacies

*Troop Sergeant Major Edwin Hughes, last survivor of the Charge of the Light Brigade, died at Blackpool in 1927. He is buried here, the last of Tennyson's 'gallant six hundred.'*

*Billy Smart produced plans in 1961 for a £5 million, 400-acre amusement park for Blackpool modelled closely on Disneyland.*

*Blackpool's Stan Mortensen remains the only player ever to have scored a hat-trick in a Wembley FA Cup Final.*

*Frank Matcham, the architect who designed dozens of music halls and theatres across the country, including Blackpool's Opera House and Grand Theatre, was born in Devon in 1854, the year that the first music hall was built at a London pub. The Grand Theatre is known to this day as 'Matcham's masterpiece.'*

*A Poulton-le-Fylde Dog and Poultry society was formed in 1893. Its joint secretary was T. Sparrow.*

*Jimmy Edwards, of 'Whacko!' fame, wrote of Blackpool in his autobiography, 'Six of the Best,' 'Earth hath not anything to show more base/ Than this detestable and loathsome place.' He didn't like us, it seems.*

*Oscar Wilde may be one of the greatest figures in English literature but he did not impress Blackpool very much when he appeared at the*

*Theatre Royal in 1883. The audience numbered a derisory 50.*

*Two aeroplanes taking part in an air circus over Blackpool in 1935 collided and one crashed on Swainson Street. The pilot and two passengers – sisters – were killed.*

*Sporting history was made by Blackpool FC in 1960. When they played Bolton Wanderers at Bloomfield Road it was the first League match to be televised live. Unfortunately, Blackpool lost 1 – 0.*

*There have been some very odd people in Blackpool! One of the more bizarre court cases of recent years was that in 1991 of a taxi driver. Outwardly the bachelor was a perfectly respectable man but as the story of his crime unfolded, it emerged he was a pervert who dreamed of bondage and making women his sex slaves. He wrote anonymously to a married woman claiming he had a diary revealing her affair with her brother. It was a pack of lies but he made so many telephone calls and wrote so many threatening letters to her that she became terrified. When police caught up with him, they found he had detailed files on famous women such as Anna Ford and Sue Cook in this country, and Madonna, Farrah Fawcett, Jane Fonda and Meryl Streep in the United States, an array of torture and bondage instruments, naked dolls, pornography, and had drawn up sex contracts for his intended victims to sign. He signed himself Xanadu. He was sent to prison for nine months. Amazingly, he was a policeman's son. Charming!*

*Daily Mail, March 31, 1993: 'Memory man Tom Morton has had to call off his one-man show – because he can't remember his lines. Mr. Morton, who was able to recall 20,000 telephone numbers, lost his memory after falling off a ladder and banging his head while decorating his flat in Marton, Blackpool. Mr. Norton, 26, dubbed the*

*Human Phone Book said yesterday: "I have been told the partial memory loss is probably only temporary. I certainly hope so because my memory is my living. And how can I face having to remember 20,000 phone numbers again?"'*

*The biggest roller-coaster in the world opened at the Pleasure Beach in 1994. The statistics involved with the new attraction are staggering. Used in the construction of the £9 million project were 5,000 cubic metres of concrete, 1,100 tonnes of steel for stanchions and monopods and 400 tonnes of steel for the track. The cars hit 85 mph as they roar down from 235 ft.*

*One of the most infamous crimes in the recent history of Blackpool took place in 1971 on a day when London gangsters ran riot in the resort's streets and brave policeman Superintendent Gerry Richardson was shot dead. The group of gangsters, among them 'Flash Fred' Sewell, held up Preston's jewellers in the Strand and made their escape towards North Shore in a Triumph car, police in pursuit in several Panda cars. In Clevedon Road the gangsters' car stopped and Sgt. Ian Hampson was shot through the window of his police car. A Panda car driven by Det. Con. Andrew Hillis continued the chase, drove his car into Clifford Road and rammed the Triumph. P.C. Patrick Jackson in another Panda car rammed the back.*

*For nearly half a century taxi-drivers in Manchester have brought a convoy of their vehicles to Blackpool every year to give a day out to handicapped youngsters at the Pleasure Beach. Sometimes there are more than 80 taxis in the convoy, decorated with ribbons and balloons and many of the drivers wearing fancy dress.*

*Blackpool Cricket Club was formed in 1889. Its present ground and pavilion in West Park Drive were opened in 1925, the gift of Sir Lindsay Parkinson and William Parkinson*

*Times change ... A 'Mr. Gay U.K.' competition was held at Blackpool in 1989. The contest, at the Flamingo Club, was won by a 22-year-old barman from the resort.*

*Perhaps ahead of the growing environmental lobby, a Marton man in 1984 set up a windmill on top of his house to generate his own electricity. Despite opposition from the local Council, a Department of the Environment Inspector over-ruled them, saying that it had no more impact on the view than the forest of television aerials that is the norm in any street nowadays.*

*The tower which grandly tops Blackpool's Town Hall was once even more grand, for until 1966 it had a spire about 70 feet tall. It was demolished because it was too expensive to repair.*

*In 1978 naturists were given permission to use Blackpool's indoor Lido. They were allowed to use the pool for two hours on a weekday August evening. Permission for them to bathe nude on the sands had been refused.*

*A double glazing company with big ideas was refused permission in 1986 to advertise itself in 15 feet high letters from top to bottom of two sides of the Tower during the Illuminations.*

*One of the most amazing sights at the Tower in recent years came in 1984, when the mighty King Kong – 84 feet tall – was rigged to the side of the structure. The vast inflatable was winched up the side of the Tower, having been brought to the resort from San Diego, California, as part of the Tower's 90th birthday celebrations. Weighing 2,500lb, the inflatable was made of 22,750 square feet of flame-resistant vinyl-coated nylon. So popular was Kong that he stayed on the Tower for a week longer than originally planned – 17 days in total – before returning to California. Perhaps the bravest person around was Lorraine Colclough, who played the part of Fae Wray, being suspended from Kong's fangs.*

*An 'unsinkable' swimsuit was demonstrated at Blackpool in 1954. It was the work of Mark Shaw, a Morecambe man who had spent years working on the material. A fisherman in full heavy clothing with big sea boots, wearing a vest containing the buoyancy material, was brought to the top at the Norbreck Hydro on his back within seconds of him jumping in. A girl was tied in a sack and thrown into the water but immediately came to the top and floated. A man in complete Army kit with greatcoat – and a brick – floated on the water. He was unable to remain below.*

*The resort claims the dubious distinction of having been the venue of the murder committed by the last woman to be hanged in Lancashire. She was Louisa Merrifield, who with her third husband, Alfred, became housekeepers at a bungalow, 339 Devonshire Road, owned by Mrs. Sarah Anne Ricketts. The Merrifields quickly wormed their way into the affections of the widow. The easy availability at that time of rat poison, Rodine, meant they could kill her easily. The pair had convinced Mrs. Ricketts to swear out her will leaving them as joint legatees. The Merrifields were arrested and charged jointly. The jury were unable to reach a verdict on Alfred but Louisa was told by the Judge, Mr. Justice Glyn-Jones, that her crime was 'as wicked and cruel a murder as I have ever heard tell of.' She was hanged in 1953. Mrs. Ricketts was said to have been something of a tippler – rum and brandy having prevented her tasting the poison.*

*The Depression of the 1930s hit Blackpool hard. The local St John Ambulance organised first aid classes at their Hornby Road headquarters to give the out-of-work something to do.*

*The Press can be a double-edged weapon. Blackpool usually enjoys a favourable relationship with the media, but every now and again something happens which will tempt reporters to lose interest in the subject they were sent to*

*King Kong*

*The Indian Lounge in the Winter Gardens; this was demolished in 1965 to be replaced by the Planet Room.*

cover. Such was the case with a special Press preview of the Illuminations in 1978. In the first place, a donkey that was to take part in the Switch-on proceedings left a rather impressive 'donation' on the steps of the Town Hall. Then a Town Hall car that was to be used to ferry Press people through the Lights burst into flames.

After Albert Edward Briggs had been seen loitering near a Blackpool boot shop in 1905 a left boot was found to be missing. Later he called at the shop and asked if they had a right boot. The manager recognised him, the police were called, arrest took place, and after appearing before the magistrates Briggs served 21 days' hard labour.

The splendid windmill at Marton, dating to about 1840, is one of only a few remaining in the Fylde, an area that in the 19th century had so many it was known as 'windmill land.' The Marton windmill was renovated in the mid-1980s and is now an eye-catching landmark for those coming into Blackpool from the M55.

The Winter Gardens Pavilion was opened by the Lord Mayor of London in 1878. It was built on the site of Bank Hey House and its grounds.

The resort has always been a place for schemes and dreams – but some problems just won't go away. One of a rather delicate nature is the 'donations' produced by the donkeys and landau horses. One solution proposed in 1986 by the president of the Blackpool Self-Catering Holiday

*Association, Mr. Ron Taylor, was that the animals should wear what in effect were giant nappies. He wrote in the organisation's magazine, engendering massive publicity: 'There are 28 studs of donkeys with up to eight donkeys per stud licensed to trade on our beach. That is a maximum of 224 donkeys and there is ample evidence of their presence ... the donkeys and landau horses are part of the Blackpool scene and should remain so — but if their owners are not willing to accept the idea of canvas bags then they should be willing to clean up after their animals.' The same idea was revived in 1993, as shown by this cutting from the Daily Mail, March 24:*

# PIN THE NAPPY ON THE DONKEY

DONKEYS on Blackpool beach may have to wear nappies to meet EC regulations.

The six miles of sands could be in line for the blue flag for cleanliness when an effluent treatment works is completed in two years.

But the sea must be clear and the beach spotless. Tourism chiefs are considering how to achieve this and keep the rides that have entertained children since Victorian times.

Options include giving the 120 donkeys nappy-style garments; appointing an 'anti-droppings' officer; creating donkey zones away from bathing areas and confining the animal rides to special tracks.

Beach bylaws are more than 100 years old and the last 'regulations for asses on the foreshore' were made in 1942. These governed rest periods, the use of sticks or whips and a weight restriction on riders. The Blackpool Donkey Owners' Association said: 'We shall co-operate however we can with the new proposals.'

# 6

## The Things they say about Blackpool!

Here are extracts from various sources, old and new, recording how Blackpool has been regarded over 170 years:

*History, Directory and Gazetteer of the County Palatine of Lancaster:* **Baines, Volume 1, 1824.**

Blackpool is not mentioned in the old maps of the county, and its celebrity as a place of fashionable resort for the recovery of health is not of more than seventy years standing. No sea bathing place can be better situated ... no wonder will be felt that there are here frequently at the height of the season from eight hundred to a thousand visitors. Blackpool has always been frequented by persons of rank and fashion, of whom there are many to be found here in the autumn months, mixed with good company from the manufacturing districts.

Southport on the opposite side of the estuary of the Ribble, has of late risen into note as a sea bathing place, and its vicinity to Liverpool, with the facility and cheapness of the water communication by the packet boats to Scarisbrick from the interior, have combined to increase the number of its visitors; but Blackpool and Lytham are still well frequented ... At present two coaches run daily to Blackpool from Preston during the season ...

The houses of public reception, are scattered along the coast with an aspect of the Irish Sea; and in the rear are the habitations of the villagers. The cottages on the beach have considerably increased during the last few years, and they serve, with the stately mansions in the centre, to give the place, when viewed from the sea, a large and imposing appearance...

The places of amusement are not overwhelmingly numerous; a company of comedians occasionally occupy an erection, dignified with the name of a theatre, which in the time of their absence is vulgarly called a barn; and those who go to obtain pleasure generally find it either in the skill of the performers, or in the shifts to which they are driven to complete the personages of the drama. The Coffee-room, News-room, and Library, all contribute their share of amusement and information, and serve to vary the pursuits of the day ...

### *History of the County Palatine and Duchy of Lancaster:* Baines, Volume 2, 1870.

**Bispham Parish:** Of this parish the sea completely forms the western boundary; and the parish of Poulton encloses it on the north, east and south. Its limits extend eight miles from north to south, and vary from one to two miles in breadth. Leyton Heys is a detached portion of the parish situated between Layton-with-Warbreck and Great Marton, but allotted to Great Bispham when the Heys was divided between the surrounding townships by Act of Parliament.

This parish comprises 3,983 statute acres. Two streams irrigate the interior of the parish: Spen-dyke, which drains the whole of Marton Moss, whence it flows until lost in the sea near Fox Hall, at Blackpool, to the south of which it forms a large pool; and Bispham-brook, the bed of which, now covered in, was formerly the main road, east to west, through the village, which, after a short course, falls into the Wyre in Thornton...

The return of population for the whole parish exhibits an increase, from 727 in 1801 to 4,344 in 1861, due to the growth of Blackpool...

This parish contains the two townships of Bispham-with-Norbreck and Layton-with-Warbreck.

**Bispham-with-Norbreck.** This township, at the north of the parish, consists of the detached hamlets of Great and Little Bispham, and Norbreck, the houses of which are occupied by substantial yeomen. The parish church is situated at Great Bispham, whence its whitened tower is seen at a considerable distance; there is also an Independent chapel ...

**Layton-with-Warbreck.** In this township is Blackpool, which from a mere waste has become a celebrated sea-bathing place. The peaty-coloured pool which gives name to the place, is near the house called Fox Hall, once a sequestered residence of the Tildesleys, there would not have been another building in Blackpool that would bear the name of 'house' so that it must have stood the little hall among huts. Nor were the huts numerous, for many were modern in 1788. Fox Hall has passed through many hands, and is now a public house! On the verge of the sea, fenced from its precipitous banks by a white railing, is the promenade, now extending a total length of $3^1/_2$ miles, and constructed at a cost of over £50,000

Although, at low water, Blackpool is more than half-a-mile from the sea, the tide at its flood brings the briny element to the door; and even the firm fabric of the earth is here an insufficient barrier against the weighty body of waters which at the periodical flow roll against the beach.

About seventy years ago there was no provision dealer in the place, and at that time four dwellings were distinguished by their slated roofs. At present there is a resident population of about five thousand. The houses are chiefly built of sea-stone, a hard and fragile substance, said to be intermitted by saline particles, which must greatly deteriorate it as a material for the construction of dwellings...

At the south end of Layton-with-Warbreck is Southshore, a village which has sprung up within the last thirty years, and has now become a part of the great watering-place of Blackpool...

The parish of Bispham, though presenting so fine a line of coast, is destitute of commerce, and its manufacturers have never exceeded a few calicos woven by the country people, to fill up the leisure hours of winter, when outdoor labour was suspended, and when the visitors to the sea coast did not require their services...

### *Blackpool Gazette and News,* July 24, 1894

Blackpool may now justifiably boast that no other watering place in the world offers such facilities for the recreation and enjoyment of its visitors. But it is not very many years since Blackpool was entirely dependent on what may be described as itinerant entertainers for the amusement of its summer visitors. But we have now got very far beyond that stage, and we may already claim that for at least three months of the year, no place in the kingdom, and we will not even except London, can offer the sight-seer so much for so small an expenditure of the current coin of the realm. Yesterday another 100 was added to the long list of Blackpool's places of resort, and Mr. Thos Sergenson, who has long been a spirited entrepreneur for the visiting masses,must be very heartily congratulated upon the enterprise which has its consummation in the New Grand Theatre and Opera House — admitted on all hands to be undoubtedly one of the finest theatres in the provinces.

Mr. Frank Matcham, the well-known theatrical architect, of 9 Warwick Court, London, was in the first instance given carte blanche, and as a result of his labours there can be no question that the new Grand Theatre is about as near perfection as architectural skill can make it, and well deserves the title 'Matcham's Masterpiece.'

The circular entrance at the corner of Church street is a fine example of stonework, and the dome and minaret cannot fail to attract the attention of all passing by. The entrance hall is prettily finished off with decorative ferneries and rockeries, while a handsome marble staircase leads to the dress circle and boxes, of which there are eight in number. Entrance to the stalls is gained by a passage leading direct from the hall, and the seats, which close up automatically immediately the spectator rises, are upholstered in blue English velvet.

The great width of the theatre finds room for a most spacious pit, and upon the parquet floor there must be sitting room for at least a thousand

*The Grand Theatre in the 1920s*

persons. The dress circle is certain to be a most popular part of the house. The upholstered tip-up seats provide for about a hundred and sixty, and behind there is a spacious saloon, charmingly decorated, together with a promenade which will provide standing room for many more.

The upper circle will easily seat from four hundred to five hundred, and here again the upholstery is in accord with the other parts of the house. The gallery will provide accommodation for at least one thousand, the view of the stage from every part being uninterrupted, so that not so far short of three thousand persons may witness the performance at one time, all seated. There are handsome crushrooms, foyers, and saloons, all parts of the house having separate retiring rooms, comfortably furnished and fitted with every convenience.

The sanitary arrangements and ventilation are up to date in every particular, and special attention has been paid to the heating apparatus, by which the whole building can be warmed to any extent in winter. Hydrant and fittings for protection from fire are placed in convenient positions, while the electric light has been installed throughout.

The fact that there are no columns to obstruct the view in any part of the house is a splendid feature of the building, and is accounted for by the fact that the framework, which is entirely of steel and of immense strength, is on the cantilever principle. The stage is a large one, and capable of staging any of the largest operas or dramas 'on the road.' Large scene docks, property rooms, etc., are arranged in conjunction. Special attention has been given to the dressing rooms; these are large, well arranged, and ventilated, comfortably furnished, heated, and fitted with enamelled slate tables; lavatories, with hot and cold water laid on. Retiring rooms, with bath and every convenience, are also provided, and these rooms are so placed that the artistes can make their entrance without crossing the stage.

We have not yet referred to the decoration of the ceiling, the fine proscenium or the fronts of the dress circle or upper circle tiers which are all of a particularly chaste and elegant character. Encircling the proscenium arch are twelve small floral panels representing the months of the year. The background is cream, but gold is lavishly used, and blue — which is the prevailing colour throughout the theatre — is introduced with charming effect. At either side there are two magnificently-painted panels which do the artists every credit. The ceiling is also divided into panels radiating from the fine centre-piece from which hang the magnificent brass electroliers, and upon these panels are inscribed in letters of gold the names of famous composers, including Sullivan, Lecocq, Collier, Soloman, Herve, Offenbach, etc.

Cream and gold are also the predominant colours in the beautiful plasterwork encircling the fronts of the upper tiers, while these are also relieved by prettily painted panels. The appearance of the stage front from any part of the house is most beautiful and the Grand deserves to rank as one of the handsomest theatres in the provinces, and we do not doubt that both residents and visitors will make haste to speedily see it for themselves.

The excavations, brickwork, sewering, etc., were carried out by Messrs. Cardwell Brothers, Blackpool. The joinery work was left to Mr. Wallworth, Gorton. The plaster decorations of the interior were provided by the Plastic Decoration Company, Strand, London, and those of the entrance hall by Messrs. Godall and Sons, London. The ironwork is from the foundry of Foster Brothers, Preston. The marble staircases, etc., are the work of Messrs. Gunn and Company, Edinburgh, while the mosaic floorings have been carried out by Bell and Sons of Lancaster. The plumbing and sanitary arrangements were in the hands of Mr. G. Coop, Ashton-under-Lyne, and other depart-ments of work may be summarised as follows: plastering, Mr. J. Whiteside, Blackpool; electricians, Sharp and Kent, London; chairs and seating, Dean and Company, Birmingham; upholsterers, Brookfield and Wyndham; fireproof curtain and stage gas apparatus, W. Tollerton, Leeds; art decorations, Binns and Sons, Halifax; fireproof floors and staircases, Hindley and Company, Manchester; heating apparatus, Mason and Company, Manchester: the whole of the stagework has been carried out by Mr. Sergenson's own workmen, and the scenery has been painted by Messrs. Dugan, Egerton and Gordon. The clerk of the works, who has efficiently superintended the erection of the whole building throughout, was Mr. G. Webber.

## *A History of Lancashire*: Lt. Col. Henry Fishwick, 1894.

On all sides the growth of trade was calling into existence new villages and towns, and the rapidly increasing number of wealthy families led to the formation of that now world-renowned place of resort — Blackpool. Here, in 1750, there were a few scattered clay-built cottages with thatched roofs, which could by no effort of imagination be called a village, when one Ethart Whiteside ventured to open a house of entertainment, which consisted of a long

Talbot Square, North Pier, Blackpool

thatched building, which he subsequently converted into an inn. Nineteen years afterwards there were only in its neighbourhood twenty or thirty cottages, but not a single shop.

In 1788 W. Hutton records that 'about sixty houses grace the sea; it does not merit the name of a village, because they are scattered to the extent of a mile;' yet in August of that year there were 400 visitors; and for their entertainment there were bowling greens, "butts for bow shooting," and many of the company amused themselves with fine ale at Number Three; and for the evening the threshing-floor of a barn was turned in to

*Talbot Square in the 1920s. The trams in the foreground are for the Circular Tour. The scene is what, in those days, would have been called 'animated'.*

a theatre... Of bathing machines there were but few; a bell was rung when ladies went to bathe, and if, during the time set apart for them, a gentleman was seen on the beach, he was fined a bottle of wine.

The price charged for boarding at one of these hotels was 3s. 4d. a day.

From this date the progress of this town was very rapid, and it soon became the great fashionable resort (during the season), of not only Lancashire, but all the North of England.

### *Our Wonderful World:* Ed. J.A. Hammerton, Amalgamated Press Ltd., Volume 3, late 1920s.

M. Eiffel was quickly destined to have a rival, and his tower had not been opened three years before foundations were laid for the erection of one at Blackpool. This tower, with the spacious building at its base, forms one of the principal attractions of this popular watering-place. The tower is certainly a symmetrical edifice, towering 520 ft. in height, a conspicuous landmark for miles around.

Unlike its counterpart in Paris, it is built of steel, 2,493 tons of this material being requisitioned in its construction. It has five tiers or platforms easily reached by lift. On the lower one are shops and restaurants, there being accommodation on these platforms for upwards of a thousand people at a time. From these vantage points magnificent views of the surrounding country may be had, the Isle of Man being distinctly visible on a clear day.

The original cost of the tower and its buildings was £400,000, and an average £500 a year is spent upon the upkeep of the tower alone. The tower buildings are unique in their arrangement, inasmuch as they contain one of the finest ball-rooms in the kingdom, a Chinese tea-room, lounges, aviary, aquarium, the only permanent circus in this country, theatre, cinema, billiard saloon and other features.

The colossal towers *(here Hammerton is referring to the country generally)* were followed by the erection of giant wheels, and then came the switchback railways and a host of other monster devices, no exhibition being complete without its amusement section with its aggregation of 'thrillers.' The Big Wheels were not altogether a financial success and many of them have been demolished. Blackpool pulled her Big Wheel down in 1929. It was modelled on the lines of one which ran for years in the grounds of the exhibition at Earl's Court, London...

*Blackpool before the First World War, when sailing boats were the order of the day. The view is from the Central Pier – note the Gigantic Wheel, on the right, dismantled at the end of the 1928 season.*

## *This Unknown Island,* S.P.B. Mais, Putnam, 1932.

Have you ever thought of taking a holiday in Lancashire? I don't mean Blackpool, although after Brighton, Blackpool is the most alive and most amusing sea-side resort I know. I don't mean Blackpool for two reasons. One is that the herding instinct, that drives the majority of people to take their holidays in a mob and share a beach with about ten thousand other people, needs no encouragement. It needs active discouragement, for it is a sign of an unreasonable dread, induced by modern industrial conditions, of being alone. Far too many people are more afraid of finding themselves alone than children are of being left in the dark. That is my first reason for not talking about Blackpool.

It is not because I don't like it. I do. I have a deep affection for Blackpool. For a day's outing or a choir-treat there's no place to tough it.

When I first came down from Oxford, I lived for four years within half a dozen miles of it — and I used to go into Blackpool as often as I could. It was a good change from a classroom. My second reason for not talking about Blackpool is that its hinterland is not attractive. The South Downs at the back of Brighton are the smoothest and most soothing little hills in England, but the region known as the Fylde is not what I should call soothing.

## 'A Seaside Place of Interest'

*The photograph opposite is taken from a book published in 1899 by Geo. Newnes Ltd. called 'Round the Coast: An Album of Pictures from Photographs of the Chief Seaside Place of Interest in Great Britain and Ireland'.*

*The caption states: 'Blackpool has two piers and everything handsome about her. Both the piers are large; the north one is the more select, and the south the more popular – just a penny pier where dancing goes on all day in the summer. In this Lancashire watering-place, there are theatres, a Grand Opera House, numerous concert halls, an aquarium, a circus, a menagerie, fine winter gardens, and other places of public assemblies, where concerts, fireworks, and all sorts of entertainments will be found duly provided. The Royal Palace Gardens, commonly known as Raike's Hall, seem to be the most popular favourite among these resorts. The promenade is lighted by electricity, and has an electric tramway.*

*Not to be left behind in any respect, Blackpool now has an Eiffel Tower of its own, which looks down upon a busy scene of enjoyment that suggests a fair rather than a seaside resort. A rate was raised for the purpose of giving these attractions wide advertisement through the medium of handbills and flaring posters; one would hardly think, however, that this was the best way of drawing the most satisfactory class of visitors to "the finest promenade in England."*

*Blackpool is a popular resort in every sense of the term; people visit it with the avowed intention of enjoying themselves to their hearts' content; and that they are successful in this respect is proclaimed by the mighty crowds that flock thither season after season, never tiring of the almost uproarious merriment that characterises the famous Lancashire watering-place'.*

# 6

# MAIN SOURCES

*History, Directory and Gazetteer of the County Palatine of Lancaster*, Baines, 1824, and later editions.

*Our Wonderful World*, Ed. J.A. Hammerton, Amalgamated Press Ltd

*Lancashire and the Lakes*, Frank Singleton, Oliver and Boyd, 1964

*This England*, National Geographic Society, 1966

*A History of Lancashire*, Lt. Col Henry Fishwick, 1894

*Directory of Westmorland and Lonsdale with Amounderness*, P Mannex 1851

*The King's England: Lancashire*, Arthur Mee, Hodder and Stoughton, 4th impression, May, 1949

*A History of Lancashire*, J.J. Bagley, Phillimore, 6th edition, 1976

*This Unknown Island*, S.P.B. Mais, Putnam, 1932

*The Face of England: A Book of the Shires and Counties*, W.S. Shears, Spring Books.

*The English Counties*, Ed. C.E.M. Joad, Odhams, reprinted 1949

*Wakes Seaside Resorts*, Ron Freethy, Faust, 1986

*The Shell Guide to England*, Ed. John Hadfield, Book Club Associates, 1977

*West Lancs Evening Gazette*, to date

*Lancashire Evening Post*, to date

*Garstang Courier*, to date

*Blackpool Herald*

*Daily Telegraph*, to date

*Preston Guardian*

*Lancashire Evening Telegraph*, to date

*Morecambe Visitor*, to date

*Fresh Air and Fun: A Blackpool Miscellany*, Ed. Bob Dobson and Doreen Bortherton, Landy Publishing, 1988

*The Motor Makers*, Martin Adeney, Collins, 1988

*Jaguar: The History of a Great British Car*, Andrew Whyte, published by Patrick Stevens

*The History of Lancashire County Council 1889 – 1974*, ed J.D. Marshall, published by Martin Robertson.

*Edwardian Blackpool: With Excursions to Fleetwood and Lytham*, G.S. Palmer and B.R. Turner, published by the authors.

*The Buildings of England: North Lancashire*, Nikolaus Pevsner, Penguin

*British Railways Past and Present: No 3 – The North West*, Paul Shannon and John Hillmer, Silver Link Publishing

*Historical and Descriptive Account of Blackpool and Its Neighbourhood*, Rev. William Thornber, 1837, republished Blackpool and Fylde Historical Society, 1985, as *The History of Blackpool and Its Neighbours.*

*Empires, Hippodromes and Palaces*, Jack Read, Alderman Press, 1986.

*Round the Coast: An album of Pictures from Photographs of the Chief Seaside Places of Interest in Great Britain and Ireland*, Geo. Newnes Ltd., 1899.

Many of the pictures in *Reflections on Blackpool* are taken from old picture postcards, some of which were loaned by Mr. Frank Brook, of Morecambe, and Mr. David Flaxington, of Heysham, to whom my thanks are recorded here. Others have been given to the writer over many years. The modern pictures are by the writer.

# Also Available from Book Clearance Centre:

# *More Book Clearance Centres are at :*

Unit 2-8, Fishergate Centre
Preston PR1 8HJ
Tel: 01772 884846

Unit 6, Marketgate Shopping Centre
Wigan WN1 1JS

Unit 28a, Town Sq. Shopping Centre
Oldham OL1 1XD
Tel: 0161 627 5244

27-28 Dawson Way, St. Johns Shopping Precinct
Liverpool L1 1LH
Tel: 0151 708 5176

7 The Mall, Millgate Shopping Centre
Bury BL9 OQQ
Tel: 0161 763 5700

47 The Concourse, Southway
Skelmersdale WN8 6LT
Tel: 01695 557817